# ATTITUDES, PERSONALITY, and BEHAVIOR

## Icek Ajzen

OPEN UNIVERSITY PRESS
MILTON KEYNES

Open University Press
Celtic Court
22 Ballmoor
Buckingham MK18 1XW

First Published 1988
Reprinted 1991, 1996

British Library Cataloguing in Publication Data

Ajzen, Icek
    Attitudes, personality, and behavior.
    (Mapping of social psychology).
    1. Social psychology
    I. Title
    II. Series
    302
    ISBN 0-335-15854-4
    ISBN 0-335-15342-9 Pbk

Typeset by Rowland Phototypesetting Limited
Bury St Edmunds, Suffolk
Printed in Great Britain by J. W. Arrowsmith Limited, Bristol

# ATTITUDES,
# PERSONALITY,
# and
# BEHAVIOR

Books are to be returned on or before
the last date below.

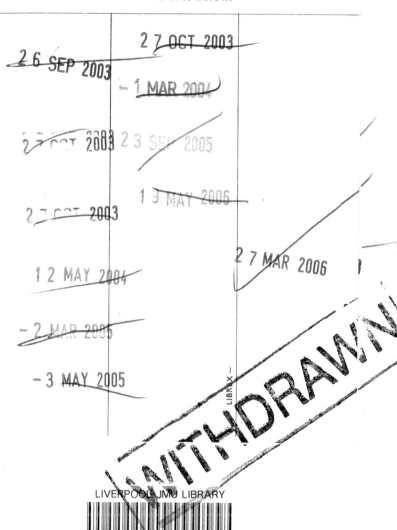

MAPPING SOCIAL PSYCHOLOGY

Series Editor: Tony Manstead

*Current titles*:

*Forthcoming titles include*:

In Memory of My Father,
Mendel Ajzen,
and of My Son Elie

# CONTENTS

# FOREWORD

There has long been a need for a carefully tailored series of reasonably short and inexpensive books on major topics in social psychology, written primarily for students by authors who enjoy a reputation for the excellence of their research and their ability to communicate clearly and comprehensibly their knowledge of, and enthusiasm for, the discipline. My hope is that the *Mapping Social Psychology* series will meet that need.

The rationale for this series is twofold. First, conventional textbooks are too low-level and uninformative for use with senior undergraduates or graduate students. Books in this series address this problem partly by dealing with topics at book length, rather than chapter length, and partly by the excellence of the scholarship and clarity of the writing. Each volume is written by an acknowledged authority on the topic in question, and offers the reader a concise and up-to-date overview of the principal concepts, theories, methods and findings relating to that topic. Although the intention has been to produce books that will be used by senior level undergraduates and graduate students, the fact that the books are written in a straightforward style should make them accessible to students with relatively little previous experience of social psychology. At the same time, the books are sufficiently informative to earn the respect of researchers and instructors.

A second problem with traditional textbooks is that they are too dependent on research conducted in or examples drawn from North American society. This fosters the mistaken impression that social psychology is a uniquely North American discipline and can also be baffling for readers unfamiliar with North American culture. To

combat this problem, authors of books in this series have been encouraged to adopt a broader perspective, giving examples or citing research from outside North America wherever this helps to make a point. Our aim has been to produce books for a world market, introducing readers to an international discipline.

The present volume does an admirable job of fulfilling the objectives I had in producing the series. Icek Ajzen is well known and highly respected for his theoretical work and empirical research on attitudes and behavior. In this book he has expanded his treatment of attitudes and behavior to include consideration of the relation between personality traits and behavior. The parallels between attitudes and personality traits as predictors of behavior are systematically explored. The evolving literatures on the attitude–behavior relationship and the trait–situation controversy are reviewed and it is shown how efforts to resolve problems in each area have followed parallel paths and point to similar conclusions. To integrate topics in social and personality psychology in this way is an instructive reminder that researchers in these fields have common concerns. The book should serve as a first-class introduction to the topic of predicting behavior from measures of dispositions such as attitudes and traits. However, this book is more than a text. In proposing his own Theory of Planned Behavior as a resolution of the classic problems of behavioral prediction, Professor Ajzen also makes a scholarly contribution. Finally, the book is a pleasure to read; the issues dealt with are complex and the theoretical analyses are sophisticated but the writing is consistently lucid and the style is engaging. It is a book that is likely to be used and enjoyed by students and researchers alike.

Tony Manstead
*Series Editor*

# PREFACE

It is a rare event in the increasingly fractured field of psychology to observe the convergence of two distinct research traditions. Such is currently the case in personality and social psychology, two areas of theory and research that started out together but drifted far apart over the years. Where not too long ago there was little communication between scientists working in these two domains, the impact of one domain on the other is now clearly felt. Methods and research findings in one area are incorporated into the other, and once-separate training programs are united to reflect the growing communality of interests. Nowhere is this convergence more readily apparent than in recent developments concerning the dispositional prediction of human behavior. Personality theorists and social psychologists are rediscovering the affinity between traits and attitudes, the central concepts in their respective fields; and they are becoming aware that the vicissitudes of these concepts have followed remarkably similar lines.

The present book on the dispositional prediction of human behavior is written in the spirit of these developments. I have tried to highlight the similarities in the way traits and attitudes are defined, in the way they are measured, and in the implications of these definitions and measurement procedures for dispositional prediction of behavior. In reviewing the literature I have drawn equally from the personality and social psychology domains. I have tried to show how, in light of poor empirical evidence for consistency, enthusiastic acceptance of the trait and attitude concepts gave way, in both domains, to rather pessimistic assessments of the validity and practical utility of the dispositional approach. And I have traced more recent parallel developments in the two domains that have resulted in the adoption of very similar solutions to the consistency dilemma, and in the re-establishment of traits and attitudes as central constructs in personality and social psychology.

In reviewing the developments of the last 20 years, I have also discussed, whenever appropriate, the contributions of my own work on the attitude–behavior relation. I have given these contributions undoubtedly more weight than they deserve, and I know that my own biases are felt throughout the book. My only excuse for this license is the advice of the series editor to contributing authors to "put a personal stamp" on their books.

Work in preparation for this book occupied much of my sabbatical year at the Hebrew University of Jerusalem. I am very grateful for the support I received from the Hebrew University and especially from its library and the Department of Psychology where I had my office. While in Jerusalem, I benefited greatly from the many fruitful discussions I had with Yaacov Trope; I appreciate his thoughtful comments very much. I would also like to thank Sy Epstein for his valuable critique of a chapter that served as the basis for this book, and Mark Snyder who read the whole manuscript and provided a very useful independent perspective. Finally, I would like to express my sincere appreciation to the series editor, Tony Manstead, for his support, encouragement, and helpful comments at various stages of the project.

*Icek Ajzen*

# 1 / ATTITUDES AND PERSONALITY TRAITS

Behavior is a mirror in which everyone shows his image.
*Goethe*

It is common practice for psychologists and laypersons alike to explain human behavior by reference to stable underlying dispositions (cf. Campbell, 1963; Heider, 1958). When people are caught lying or cheating they are considered dishonest; when they perform poorly they are said to lack ability or motivation; when they help a person in need they are called altruistic or compassionate; and when they discriminate against members of a minority group they are termed prejudiced.

Dispositional explanations of behavior have a long and distinguished history in personality and social psychology. In the domain of personality psychology the *trait* concept has carried the burden of dispositional explanation. A multitude of personality traits has been identified – among them dominance, sociability, independence, conscientiousness, hostility, helpfulness, self-esteem, emotional stability, ambitiousness – and new trait dimensions continue to join the growing list. In a similar fashion the concept of *attitude* has been the focus of attention in explanations of human behavior offered by social psychologists. Numerous attitudes have been assessed over the years and, as new social issues emerge, additional attitudinal domains are explored. Examples are attitudes toward the church, toward hospitals and doctors, toward smoking and drinking, toward open education, toward politicians and political parties, toward ethnic groups and nationalities, and toward a host of social issues, such as nuclear power, energy conservation, protection of the environment, and the like.

This book is, at the most general level, concerned with the usefulness of the trait and attitude constructs. Following a brief discussion of the ways in which these dispositions have been conceptualized and measured, we examine the extent to which people in fact act in accordance with their traits and attitudes. We will see that correspondence between measured dispositions and overt actions is not as simple a matter as it might at first appear, and we will discuss some of the factors that have been found to influence the degree of correspondence that can be expected. This review and integration of the relevant literature in personality and social psychology is followed by a presentation of a theoretical model that offers a general framework for dispositional prediction and explanation of social behavior.

## From acts to dispositions

How do we know that a person is outgoing or reclusive, honest or dishonest, dominant or submissive; that s/he opposes or favors greater political integration of Europe, approves or disapproves of abortion, likes or dislikes the Prime Minister? We cannot observe these traits and attitudes, they are not part of a person's physical characteristics, nor do we have direct access to the person's thoughts and feelings. Clearly, personality traits and attitudes are latent, hypothetical characteristics that can only be *inferred* from external, observable cues. The most important such cues are the individual's behavior, verbal or nonverbal, and the context in which the behavior occurs (cf. Heider, 1958; Jones and Davis, 1965; Kelley, 1971).

### Inferring personality traits from behavior

A personality trait is defined as a characteristic of an individual that exerts pervasive influence on a broad range of trait-relevant responses. Assumed to be behavioral manifestations of an underlying trait, people's responses are taken as indications of their standing on the trait in question. Table 1.1 shows that trait-relevant information can come from three sources: an observer, the individual him- or herself, or other people familiar with the individual, such as friends, parents, or peers. Of course, many different kinds of responses can be considered manifestations of an underlying personality characteristic. Table 1.1 indicates that the responses used to infer a trait can be overt, i.e. directly observable, or covert, i.e. not directly accessible to

*Table 1.1* Responses used to infer personality traits

| Nature of response | Source of information about responses | | |
| --- | --- | --- | --- |
| | Observation | Person | Acquaintances |
| Overt | Motor acts, nonverbal cues, verbal behavior | Self-reports of motor acts, nonverbal cues | Peer-reports of motor acts, nonverbal cues |
| Covert | Physiological responses | Self-reports of thoughts, feelings, needs, desires | Peer-reports of thoughts, feelings, needs, desires |

an outside observer, although some covert responses, such as changes in blood pressure or heart rate, can be assessed by means of appropriate instruments.

Consider, for example, extraversion or the extent to which a person is outgoing. To infer a person's standing on this trait, we could examine overt behaviors in social situations, such as the number of interactions with others in a given time interval, the number of telephone calls made, the number of conversations with strangers initiated in the course of a week, or the number of words emitted during a 15-minute conversation with another person. In addition, we could consider such nonverbal cues as amount of eye contact with a conversation partner or seating distance from other people. Alternatively, we might direct our attention to internal reactions such as changes in heart rate or blood pressure when addressed by a stranger. Each of these reactions to other people could be taken as an indication of a person's degree of extraversion or introversion.

Of course, observing overt behaviors or internal reactions as they occur in naturalistic settings is costly and time-consuming. Mainly for practical reasons, therefore, personality inventories often rely on self-reports of behavior, or reports provided by others familiar with the individual. Thus, we can ask people about the number of friends they have, how often they initiate conversations with strangers, how many parties they attend, how they feel in the presence of others, and so on. In addition to direct questions of this kind, we can also use disguised techniques that approach the inference process in a covert manner. Among the better known examples are responses to ink blots (the Rorschach method) or ambiguous pictures (the Thematic Apperception Test, or TAT). Appropriate analyses of these responses may reveal deep-seated fears of other people or needs to affiliate, which provide cues about the degree of introversion or extraversion. Finally, we can ask a person's acquaintances to provide information about overt or covert responses relevant to sociability: how much the person likes parties, how many close friends s/he has, the extent to which s/he is shy in front of others, and so forth. Like observations of overt behaviors or nonverbal cues, self-reports or reports provided by acquaintances can be taken as indications of a person's standing on the underlying sociability trait.

## Inferring attitudes from behavior

An attitude is a disposition to respond favorably or unfavorably to an object, person, institution, or event. Although formal definitions of attitude vary, most contemporary social psychologists seem to agree that the characteristic attribute of attitude is its evaluative (pro–con, pleasant–unpleasant) nature (see, e.g. Bem, 1970; Edwards, 1957; Fishbein and Ajzen, 1975; Hill, 1981; Osgood et al., 1957; Oskamp, 1977). This view is strengthened by the fact that, as we shall see below, standard attitude scaling techniques result in a score that locates an individual on an evaluative dimension vis-à-vis the attitude object (cf. Fishbein and Ajzen, 1975; Green, 1954).

Like personality trait, attitude is a hypothetical construct that, being inaccessible to direct observation, must be inferred from measurable responses. Given the nature of the construct, these responses must reflect positive or negative evaluations of the attitude object. Beyond this requirement, however, there is virtually no limitation on the kinds of responses that can be considered. To simplify matters, it is useful to categorize attitude-relevant responses into various subgroups. Thus, we might distinguish between responses directed at others and responses directed at the self, between behaviors performed in public and behavior performed in private, or between actions and reactions. However, the most popular classification system goes back at least to Plato and distinguishes between three categories of responses: cognition, affect, and conation (see Allport, 1954; Hilgard, 1980; and McGuire, 1969 for general discussions). Within each of these categories, it is also useful to

*Table 1.2*  Responses used to infer attitudes

| Response mode | Response category | | |
|---|---|---|---|
| | *Cognition* | *Affect* | *Conation* |
| Verbal | Expressions of beliefs about attitude object | Expressions of feelings toward attitude object | Expressions of behavioral intentions |
| Non-verbal | Perceptual reactions to attitude object | Physiological reactions to attitude object | Overt behaviors with respect to attitude object |

separate verbal from nonverbal responses. Based on Rosenberg and Hovland's (1960) analysis, Table 1.2 shows the different types of responses from which attitudes can thus be inferred.

*Cognitive responses*

In the first category are responses that reflect perceptions of, and information about, the attitude object. To illustrate, consider some of the responses we might use to infer attitudes toward the medical profession. Cognitive responses of a verbal nature are expressions of *beliefs* that link the medical profession with certain characteristics or attributes. Beliefs to the effect that physicians are mostly interested in money, that hospitals are overcrowded, that many health profession-als are poorly qualified, or that most diseases cannot be cured by traditional methods, might be taken as evidence of a negative attitude toward the medical profession. By way of contrast, a favorable attitude would be implied by expressions of beliefs sug-gesting that nurses and doctors do their best to help patients, that medicine has made considerable progress over the years, that many physicians work long and inconvenient hours, and the like.

Cognitive responses of a nonverbal kind are more difficult to assess, and the information they provide about attitudes is usually more indirect. For example, we might argue that people with favor-able attitudes toward the medical establishment have relatively low thresholds for the perception of attitude-relevant positive stimuli, whereas people with unfavorable attitudes have relatively low thresholds for negative stimuli. To infer attitudes toward the medical profession, therefore, we might measure how long it takes a person to appreciate the significance of cartoons depicting doctors, nurses and hospitals in either a favorable or an unfavorable light.

### Affective responses

The second category of responses from which attitudes can be inferred has to do with evaluations of, and feelings toward, the attitude object. Here again, we can distinguish between affective responses of a verbal and of a nonverbal kind. Verbal affective responses with respect to the medical profession, for example, can be expressions of admiration or disgust, appreciation or disdain. Thus, a person who claims to admire physicians or nurses, or to "feel good" about the available medical care, would seem to hold a favorable attitude toward the medical profession, but a person who indicates that the mere thought of doctors and hospitals is disgusting would seem to hold a negative attitude.

Facial expressions, as well as various physiological and other bodily reactions, are often assumed to reflect affect in a nonverbal mode. Among the bodily reactions considered are the galvanic skin response (electrical conductance of the skin), constriction and dilation of the pupil, heart rate, the reactions of facial muscles, and other reactions of the sympathetic nervous system. One of the difficulties inherent in methods that rely on responses of this kind is the problem of distinguishing between reactions that imply favorable attitudes and reactions that imply unfavorable attitudes, although recent research has reported some progress in this regard (see Cacioppo et al., 1986b).

### Conative responses

Responses of a conative nature are behavioral inclinations, intentions, commitments, and actions with respect to the attitude object. Starting again with the verbal mode of expression, we can consider what people say they do, plan to do, or would do under appropriate circumstances. Thus, people with negative attitudes toward the medical profession might indicate that they would refuse to be hospitalized, that they see a doctor only when absolutely necessary, or that they discourage their children from going to medical school. Those with positive attitudes, on the other hand, might express intentions to donate money to a fund for a new hospital wing, they might plan to encourage their children to go to medical school, they might indicate a readiness to read about advances in medicine, and so on.

Nonverbal conative responses indicating favorable or unfavorable attitudes toward the medical profession are also easily imagined. Thus, people who actually read books or articles about medicine, who encourage their children to go to medical school, or who accept and follow their physicians' advice would be classified as having positive attitudes, whereas people who refuse to donate money to a medical fund or who write letters to newspapers complaining about the medical profession would be said to have negative attitudes.

In sum, an individual's favorable or unfavorable attitude toward an object, institution, or event can be inferred from verbal or nonverbal responses toward the object, institution, or event in question. These responses can be of a cognitive nature, reflecting perceptions of the object, or beliefs concerning its likely characteristics; they can be of an affective nature, reflecting the person's evaluations and feelings; and they can be of a conative nature, indicating how a person does or would act with respect to the object.

## Attitudes versus traits

For the most part, the present book emphasizes the similarities of the trait and attitude concepts. There are, however, also some important differences between traits and attitudes that we should briefly consider. Clearly, both terms refer to latent, hypothetical constructs that manifest themselves in a wide variety of observable responses. In the case of attitudes, these responses are evaluative in nature and they are directed at a given object or target (a person, institution, policy, or event). Personality traits, by contrast, are not necessarily evaluative. They describe response tendencies in a given domain, such as the tendency to behave in a conscientious manner, to be sociable, to be self-confident, etc. The responses that reflect an underlying trait do not focus on any particular external target. Instead, they focus on the individual him- or herself and they can thus be used to differentiate between individuals and to classify them into different personality types. Although attitudes and traits are both assumed to be relatively stable, enduring dispositions, attitudes are typically viewed as more malleable than personality traits. Evaluations can change rapidly as events unfold and new information about a person or issue becomes available, but the configuration of personality traits that characterizes an individual is much more resistant to transformation.

*Assessment procedures*

The discussion of attitude and personality measurement in this section is not intended to provide a thorough treatment of the subject. Many methods are available, some quite sophisticated in terms of the stimulus situations they create, the ways they assess responses, and the statistical procedures they employ. [Interested readers can consult Edwards (1957), Fishbein and Ajzen (1975) and Green (1954) for the construction of attitude scales, and Jackson (1971), Kleinmuntz (1967) and Wiggins (1973) for personality assessment.] The purpose of the present treatment is merely to introduce the reader to some of the basic principles involved in the assessment of dispositions, especially those principles that have some bearing on our discussions in later chapters of attitude–behavior and trait–behavior relations.

Most methods used to infer traits or attitudes rely on verbal responses to questionnaire items. Our discussion of trait and attitude measurement will therefore focus on verbal responses, but it should be kept in mind that the same procedures can be applied equally well to observations of nonverbal responses. Furthermore, our discussion will be concerned primarily with self-reports of behavior or of internal states, rather than with reports provided by others familiar with the individual. Again, however, the methods discussed can be applied just as well to peer-reports as to self-reports.

*Direct assessment*

**Single items**   The simplest procedure in many ways is to ask respondents to report directly on their own attitudes or personality traits. Many studies in personality and social psychology have employed direct probes of this kind. Consider the following recent examples.

In a study dealing with the effect of vested interest on the attitude–behavior relation, Sivacek and Crano (1982) used a 7-point scale to assess attitudes of college students toward raising to 21 the legal drinking age in the State of Michigan (where the study was conducted). The scale took the following form:

Michigan's drinking age should be raised to 21
agree :__:__:__:__:__:__:__: disagree

In another study of the attitude–behavior relation, Lord *et al.* (1984) assessed, among other things, attitudes toward homosexuals. Respondents were asked to rate, on a 10-point scale, how likeable they found the typical homosexual. The investigators did not report the exact details of the scale, but it could have looked as follows:

Homosexuals are

extremely                                              not at all
likeable  :__:__:__:__:__:__:__:__:__: likeable

Chaiken and Yates (1985) used two single items, each involving an 11-point scale, to obtain direct measures of attitudes toward capital punishment and toward censorship, as follows:

I favor                                              I oppose
capital                                            capital pun-
punishment :__:__:__:__:__:__:__:__:__:__: ishment


I favor                                              I oppose
censorship :__:__:__:__:__:__:__:__:__:__: censorship

Comparable examples can be found in the personality domain. Thus, in a study by Monson *et al.* (1982) that dealt with the introversion–extraversion trait, undergraduate college students were given the following descriptions of extraverts and introverts:

Extraverts are typically outgoing, sociable, energetic, confident, talkative, and enthusiastic. Generally confident and relaxed in social situations, this type of person rarely has trouble making conversation with others.

Introverts are typically somewhat more shy, timid, reserved, quiet, distant, and retiring. Often this type of person is relatively awkward or ill at ease in social situations, and consequently is not nearly as adept at making good conversation.

As a measure of introversion–extraversion, the participants were asked to indicate which was a better description of themselves.

Buss and Craik (1980) used several methods to assess the degree of dominance among a sample of college students, including a 7-point self-rating scale. The scale may have appeared in the questionnaire as follows:

I would describe myself as (check one)
___ extremely dominant
___ quite dominant
___ slightly dominant
___ neither dominant nor submissive
___ slightly submissive
___ quite submissive
___ extremely submissive


In many cases, single items of this kind have proved quite adequate for the assessment of particular attitudes or personality traits. There are, however, potential drawbacks to this method. Some of the problems are shared by other methods and will be considered later, but one issue is particularly bothersome for single-item measures of attitudes or personality traits. This is the question of *reliability*, or the extent to which repeated assessments of the same trait or attitude produce equivalent results. Single responses tend to be quite unreliable, leading to low correlations between repeated observations. Misreading a statement or placing a check mark in the wrong place can produce a response that implies extraversion or a negative attitude toward homosexuals, but on another occasion, the item may be read appropriately, and a different response is given. For this reason, and for other reasons to be discussed below, it is usually preferable to use multi-item measures of attitudes and personality traits.


**Multi-item measures**    Perhaps the best-known multi-item measure used to obtain a relatively direct indication of attitude is the *semantic differential*, developed by Osgood and his associates (Osgood *et al.*, 1957). Designed originally to measure the meaning of a concept, it is now used in a variety of contexts. As a measure of attitude, the semantic differential consists of a set of bipolar evaluative adjective pairs, such as *good–bad, harmful–beneficial, pleasant–unpleasant, desirable–undesirable*, and *awful–nice*. Each adjective pair is placed on opposite ends of a 7-point scale, and respondents are asked to mark each scale as it best reflects their evaluation of the attitude object. Thus, the following evaluative semantic differential could be used to assess attitudes toward homosexuals:

Homosexuals are

pleasant :__:__:__:__:__:__:__: unpleasant
harmful :__:__:__:__:__:__:__: beneficial
good :__:__:__:__:__:__:__: bad
awful :__:__:__:__:__:__:__: nice

Responses are scored from $-3$ on the negative side of each scale to $+3$ on the positive side, and the sum over the four scales is a measure of the respondent's attitude toward homosexuals.

In their study of attitude change mentioned earlier, Chaiken and Yates (1985) used such an evaluative semantic differential as another way of assessing attitudes toward capital punishment and toward censorship. The 4-item semantic differential with respect to capital punishment looked as follows:

Capital punishment is

good :__:__:__:__:__:__:__: bad
foolish :__:__:__:__:__:__:__: wise
sick :__:__:__:__:__:__:__: healthy
harmful :__:__:__:__:__:__:__: beneficial

A simple replacement of "Capital punishment" by "Censorship" allowed the investigators to use the same instrument to assess attitudes toward censorship.

Personality researchers have tended to use adjective checklists, rather than opposite adjective pairs, to obtain self-reports of personality traits. Consider, again, the extraversion–introversion trait mentioned earlier. In the paragraph descriptions of this trait dimension shown above, several specific adjectives were used to illustrate the two extremes: outgoing, sociable, energetic, confident, talkative, and enthusiastic versus shy, timid, reserved, quiet, distant, and retiring. This list of adjectives could be presented to respondents in random order, and they could be asked to indicate, for each adjective, how characteristic it was of them. A frequently used format asks respondents to place a number in front of each adjective, as in the following example:

5 = extremely characteristic of me
4 = quite characteristic of me
3 = neither characteristic nor uncharacteristic of me
2 = quite uncharacteristic of me
1 = extremely uncharacteristic of me

| | |
|---|---|
| ___ outgoing | ___ shy |
| ___ energetic | ___ sociable |
| ___ reserved | ___ confident |
| ___ distant | ___ talkative |
| ___ enthusiastic | ___ retiring |
| ___ quiet | ___ timid |

The respondent's degree of extraversion is computed as follows. The scores for the introverted adjectives (reserved, shy, timid, etc.) are reversed, such that 5 becomes 1, 4 becomes 2, etc., and these scores are added to the scores for the extraverted adjectives. The higher the total score, the more extraverted the respondent's self-report.

Direct measures of dispositions that rely on multiple items have fewer problems of reliability than single-item measures. Clerical mistakes and other incidental factors that affect the score on one item but not on the others will have little systematic impact on the overall score. Different kinds of errors associated with different items will tend to cancel each other out, leaving the total score relatively unaffected. The greater the number of items used, therefore, the more reliable the score will tend to be. In fact, it is possible to compute the increment in reliability that is likely to result from an increased number of items. The relationship between the number of items in our measure and its reliability is given by the Spearman-Brown prophecy formula, as shown in Equation 1.1:

$$r'_{xx'} = \frac{mr_{xx'}}{1 + (m-1)r_{xx'}}, \qquad (1.1)$$

where $r'_{xx'}$ is the estimate of reliability for a scale $m$ times as long as the original scale, and $r_{xx'}$ is the assessed reliability of the original scale.[1]* According to this formula, when a single-item measure has a relatively low reliability of, say, 0.40, a measure consisting of four items will nevertheless have a respectable reliability of 0.72.

Note that nothing was said so far about the ways in which the semantic differential scales were selected to assess attitudes toward homosexuals or toward capital punishment, nor about the ways in which extraversion–introversion adjectives were selected. Each scale on a semantic differential is supposed to reflect evaluation of the

---

* Superscript numerals refer to numbered notes at the end of each chapter.

attitude object, and each adjective on a checklist should be representative of the personality trait that is being assessed. Procedures for selecting appropriate items to be included in an attitude or personality inventory are taken up next in the discussion of indirect methods for the assessment of behavioral dispositions.

*Indirect assessment*

Direct dispositional measures of the multi-item kind have proved very useful in attitude and personality research. They are easily developed and, for this reason, are very popular, especially in the context of laboratory studies. For some purposes, however, they are somewhat limited because they may elicit relatively superficial responses. Consider, for example, attitudes toward the military. When asked to rate the military on an evaluative semantic differential, responses may reflect an image salient at the time in the person's mind. Perhaps this image was molded by television coverage of a demonstration brutally suppressed by military forces. If induced to think more thoroughly about the military, however, respondents might consider its role in the defense of their country, the educational opportunities it provides for young people who otherwise would go without this education, and so forth. Similarly, people who, in response to an adjective checklist, indicate that they are relatively conscientious might, if induced to scan their behavior more thoroughly, realize that there are many situations in which they behave less reliably than they thought they did. Indirect measures of attitudes and personality traits provide opportunities for respondents to review different aspects of a given domain. The responses they provide to a set of specific questions are then used to infer the disposition under investigation.

Earlier we discussed the different kinds of verbal responses that can be used to infer traits and attitudes (see Tables 1.1 and 1.2). Usually, the items that appear on a questionnaire are statements of beliefs, of behavioral intentions, or of actual behavior, and respondents are asked to indicate their agreement or disagreement with each statement. As an example in the attitude domain, consider the following statements taken from a 22-item scale that was developed by Rundquist and Sletto (1936) to measure attitudes toward the law.

The law protects property rights at the expense of human rights. $(-)$

On the whole, policemen are honest. $(+)$

It is all right to evade the law if you do not actually violate it.   (−)

Juries seldom understand a case well enough to make a really just decision.   (−)

In the courts a poor man will receive as fair treatment as a millionaire.   (+)

It is difficult to break the law and keep one's self-respect.   (+)

Respondents answer each item by choosing one of five alternatives, a format proposed by Likert (1932) as part of his attitude scaling method:

_____ Strongly agree

_____ Agree

_____ Undecided

_____ Disagree

_____ Strongly disagree

The scoring key for each item is shown in parentheses. Positive items are scored from 5 (strongly agree) to 1 (strongly disagree), while the reverse scoring is used for negative items. The respondent's total attitude score is computed by summing all item scores; high scores indicate positive attitudes toward the law.

A second example of an attitude scale can be found in a study of religion and humanitarianism by Kirkpatrick (1949). The following statements are a sample of the 69 items on Kirkpatrick's attitude toward religion scale.

No scientific law has yet given a satisfactory explanation of the origin of life.   (+)

The soul is a mere supposition, having no better standing than a myth.   (−)

Belief in God makes life on earth worthwhile.   (+)

Without the church there would be a collapse of morality.   (+)

The findings of modern science leave many mysteries unsolved, but they are still incompatible with a personal God concept.   (−)

The scoring key is again given in parentheses. Respondents are asked to indicate whether they agree or disagree with each statement. Agreement with a positive item is counted as +1 and disagreement as −1. For negative items, agreement is counted as −1 and disagreement as +1. Attitudes toward religion are computed by summing over all 69 items; high scores indicate positive attitudes toward religion.

Similar procedures are adopted in the personality domain to assess various personality traits. Consider, for example, Eysenck's (1956) extraversion scale. Among the 24 items on the scale are the following:

Are you inclined to keep quiet when out in a social group?   (no)
Do you like to have many social engagements?   (yes)
Would you rate yourself as a happy-go-lucky individual?   (yes)
Is it difficult to "lose yourself" even at a lively party?   (no)
Do you generally prefer to take the lead in group activities?   (yes)
Are you inclined to be shy in the presence of the opposite sex?   (no)

Respondents answer "yes," "no," or "undecided" to each question. The scoring key in the direction of extraversion is shown in parentheses after each item. An answer in accordance with the scoring key is given two points, an answer contrary to the key is given zero points, and an undecided response is given one point. The sum over all 24 items on the scale is the measure of a person's extraversion tendency.

As another example in the personality domain, consider the following items from Fenigstein *et al.*'s (1975) 10-item private self-consciousness scale. Responses to each item are given on a 5-point scale that ranges from *extremely uncharacteristic* to *extremely characteristic*. The scoring key is shown in parentheses. A plus sign indicates that the item expresses high self-consciousness, a minus sign that it expresses low self-consciousness.

I am always trying to figure myself out.   (+)
I reflect about myself a lot.   (+)
Generally, I'm not very aware of myself.   (−)
I'm alert to changes in my mood.   (+)

Responses are scored from 1 (extremely uncharacteristic) to 5 (extremely characteristic) for items expressing high self-consciousness, and in reversed fashion for items expressing low self-consciousness. The final private self-consciousness score is obtained by summing over all 10 items on the scale.

**Item selection**   In the measurement of dispositions, the most important part is the formulation of a large set of statements and selection of appropriate items from which the disposition of interest can be validly inferred. The first step in the selection procedure involves mapping the domain of the attitude or personality trait in question. We need to decide what kinds of responses we want to include in our definition of the disposition before we can construct appropriate items. For example, if we want to measure attitudes toward the European Community, we could decide to restrict our definition of the domain to economic aspects of cooperation and competition among the nations of Western Europe who are part of the Community. Alternatively, we could define the attitude object much more broadly as including cultural, political, military, and social relations among member nations. Similarly, before we can construct items for a personality measure of, say, conscientiousness, we must define the concept's domain of application. Among other things, we need to map the situations in which conscientiousness can be observed (at work, at home, with friends, etc.) as well as the different kinds of behaviors in which it can find expression (reliability, punctuality, neatness, honesty, and so on).

Once the domain is clearly defined, we can proceed with the construction of items that explore the various aspects of the domain. Of course, not every item that, on the face of it, appears to be relevant for the disposition of interest will in fact be found appropriate. For this reason the investigator usually constructs a large pool of items, perhaps as many as 100 or 200, from which the final set is selected. It is beyond the scope of this chapter to review the different item selection procedures that have been developed for the measurement of attitudes and personality traits. We will here deal only with the major considerations involved in many popular methods.

To understand the logic of item selection we must first explore the nature of attitude and personality trait scores. As we saw in the above examples of attitude scales, a respondent's answer to a given item is, depending on the nature of the item, taken as an indication of a positive or a negative attitude. The response to one item can imply a positive attitude, the response to another item a negative attitude. Only in their totality do responses to the scale reveal the respondent's overall attitude. A person who agrees with many positive items, and with few negative items, is said to have a relatively favorable attitude; a person who agrees with many negative statements and disagrees with many positive statements is said to have a relatively unfavorable attitude; and a person who agrees with about as many positive as negative items is said to have a relatively neutral attitude. Thus, the attitude score, which is computed by summing the responses to all items on the scale, reflects the *degree* to which the respondent's attitude is favorable or unfavorable.

By the same token, responses to statements on a personality scale indicate high or low standing on the personality trait being assessed. The response to one item on a scale designed to assess dominance may indicate that the person is dominant, whereas the response to another item may indicate that he is submissive. As in the case of attitudes, the respondent's location on the trait dimension can be ascertained only by considering the responses to all items on the scale. Thus, the trait score on a dominance scale indicates the *degree* to which a person is dominant or submissive.

To select the most appropriate items from the large pool constructed by the investigator, the initial pool of items is administered to a sample of respondents. Preliminary attitude or trait scores are computed by summing over all items in the pool. Assuming that the majority of items initially constructed by the investigator do indeed reflect the disposition of interest, the preliminary score will be a reasonably good first approximation and can thus serve as a criterion for item selection.[2] That is, to the extent that a given item is a good representative of the dispositional domain, it should correlate with the total score. For this reason, the item–total correlation is the most important, and most frequently used, criterion in item selection procedures. In attitude measurement, this criterion was first proposed by Likert (1932); it is known as the *criterion of internal consistency*, and it is the critical feature of the Likert scaling method (see Edwards, 1957; Green, 1954).[3]

The next step, then, in the construction of an attitude or personality scale is the selection of items from the initial pool that have the highest correlations with the total score (i.e. with the preliminary attitude or trait score). These items may be said to represent best the disposition of interest, as it is reflected in the total score. Once this criterion is met and we have a set of items that correlate highly with the total score, other considerations may enter as well. One frequently mentioned recommendation is that, in spite of their relatively high correlations with the total score, the items selected should not correlate too strongly with each other. We could obtain high correlations among all items in a pool, and hence between each item and the total score, by simply rewording the same statement in different ways. A set of statements constructed in this manner would, however, fail adequately to reflect the general attitude or trait domain under investigation. Instead, it would assess a very narrow response tendency. The requirement that items have low correlations with each other ensures a relatively heterogeneous set of items that explore the general domain, while the internal consistency criterion ensures that each item is in fact representative of that domain.

The final attitude or personality scale consists of a relatively small set of items that have passed the criteria of internal consistency and heterogeneity. This scale can now be administered to a sample of respondents, and attitude or trait scores are computed by summing over all item scores.

**Representativeness and validity**   The fact that items on an attitude or personality scale are concerned with different aspects of the dispositional domain has important implications for the representativeness and validity of our measures. It suggests that, for several reasons, no single item is likely to capture fully the attitude or personality trait of interest. Obviously, each item only deals with a limited aspect of the disposition's domain of application. Moreover, any single response is influenced by a multitude of factors, some quite unrelated to the attitude or personality trait under study. Consider, for example, the statement, "No scientific law has yet given a satisfactory explanation of the origin of life," which was part of the attitude toward religion scale mentioned earlier. Some respondents may disagree with this item, not because they hold unfavorable attitudes toward religion but because they have respect for science. Conversely, agreement with the statement may reflect dissatisfaction with the state of modern science rather than rejection of science on the basis of religious belief.

It is for these reasons that responses to single items tend to be unrepresentative and invalid measures of broad behavioral dispositions. In fact, even after meeting the criterion of internal consistency, items included on the final attitude or personality scale tend to correlate only moderately with the total score. The typical correlation between responses to any given item on a scale and the overall score tends to be in the 0.30–0.40 range. Clearly, then, by themselves, single items cannot be considered valid indicators of the underlying disposition. Only in the aggregate can responses to an attitude or personality scale be said to assess the general behavioral disposition of interest. As we aggregate responses, by summing the different item scores, we eliminate the influence of unique factors associated with any given item. These unique factors tend to "cancel out" and the total score reflects the common core of all items on the scale, namely, the attitude or personality trait that is being inferred.

## From dispositions to actions

Personality traits and attitudes are considered to be more than mere abstractions or hypothetical entities invented for the convenience of psychologists. Most theorists assume that these dispositions have an existence of their own, independent of our efforts to infer them. Indeed, once inferred, traits and attitudes are used to *explain* the person's behavior.

### Dimensions of personality

The trait approach to personality assumes that individuals can be described in terms of a perhaps large, but finite, number of personality characteristics. In line with this assumption, much research over the years has attempted to identify the primary or basic traits in human personality (e.g. Cattell, 1947; Eysenck, 1953; Jackson, 1967). The emerging consensus is that five major personality dimensions are sufficient to describe people's standing on the great variety of trait terms found in common language (see Digman and Inouye, 1986; Fiske, 1949; W. T. Norman, 1963). Table 1.3 shows the five general personality factors and lists a few examples of trait pairs that are

*Table 1.3*   Five basic personality factors (after W. T. Norman, 1963)

| | |
|---|---|
| *Factor 1:* | *Extraversion–introversion*<br>Talkative–silent, frank–secretive, adventurous–cautious, sociable–reclusive |
| *Factor 2:* | *Agreeableness*<br>Good-natured–irritable, gentle–headstrong, cooperative–negativistic, not jealous–jealous |
| *Factor 3:* | *Conscientiousness*<br>Tidy–careless, responsible–undependable, scrupulous–unscrupulous, persevering–quitting |
| *Factor 4:* | *Emotional stability*<br>Calm–anxious, composed–excitable, poised–nervous, not hypochondriacal–hypochondriacal |
| *Factor 5:* | *Culture*<br>Artistically sensitive–insensitive, imaginative–simple, intellectual–nonreflective, refined–crude |

representative of each. People's personalities are thus described quite well if we can specify how sociable, agreeable, conscientious, emotionally stable, and cultured they are. These personality characteristics are expected to find expression in behavior. For example, people who are extraverted should be talkative rather than silent, adventurous rather than cautious, sociable rather than reclusive, etc. And within each of these behavioral categories we can find still more specific response tendencies. Thus, in comparison to relatively silent individuals, talkative people should make more telephone calls, speak up more frequently in group settings, turn more to other people for assistance, and so forth. In short, the links from traits to behavior proceed from general personality characteristics to more narrowly defined behavioral tendencies which, in turn, result in relatively specific response dispositions.

## A hierarchical model of attitude

The logic whereby attitudes are linked to behavior is remarkably similar to the trait approach in personality. Earlier we saw that attitudes can be inferred from cognitive, affective, and conative responses to the attitude object. For many theorists, however, the distinction between cognition, affect, and conation is more than just a system for classifying responses from which attitudes can be inferred. These theorists assume that each response category reflects a different theoretical *component* of attitude (e.g. Katz and Stotland, 1959; Smith 1947). In this view, attitude is a multidimensional construct consisting of cognition, affect, and conation. Although each of these components varies along an evaluative continuum, it is assumed that the evaluations expressed in them can differ (see Breckler, 1984; Ostrom, 1969). A person might feel uneasy in a hospital (negative affect with respect to the medical profession) but, at the same time, believe that most doctors are well qualified (positive cognitive component) and agree to undergo an operation (favorable conative component).

The tripartite model of attitude offered by Rosenberg and Hovland (1960), which serves as the starting point of most contemporary analyses, is a hierarchical model that includes cognition, affect, and conation as first-order factors and attitude as a single second-order factor. In this model, the three components are defined independently and yet comprise, at a higher level of abstraction, the single construct of attitude. To extend this line of reasoning, recall that each component is made up of verbal and nonverbal response classes, and that each of these is further comprised of a large number of very specific response tendencies. Attitudes are thus always inferred from specific responses to the attitude object. We can classify these responses into broader categories and assign different labels to those categories, yet we are still dealing with the same evaluative disposition called attitude.

The shared evaluative character of the cognitive, affective and conative attitudinal components has sometimes been a source of confusion. This is especially apparent in attempts to distinguish empirically between cognition and affect. In fact, there is considerable disagreement as to the appropriate means of separating these two components. For example, some investigators (e.g. R. Norman, 1975) have employed the evaluative semantic differential as a measure of affect, whereas others (e.g. Breckler, 1984) have used it as a measure of cognition. Close examination of the semantic differential's evaluative factor (see Osgood *et al.*, 1957) actually reveals a mixture of what appear to be cognitive (e.g. useful–useless) and affective (e.g. pleasant–unpleasant) adjective scales. The two types of scales are often highly correlated and thus tend to reflect the same factor, but at times they are found to tap two different underlying constructs (see Ajzen and Timko, 1986). It is thus possible, by carefully selecting appropriate scales, to use the semantic differential to assess an attitude's cognitive component or its affective component.

The empirical implications of the hierarchical attitude model can be stated as follows. Given that the three components reflect the same underlying attitude, they should correlate to some degree with each other. Yet, to the extent that the distinction between cognitive, affective, and conative response categories is of psychological significance, measures of the three components should not be completely redundant. In combination, these expectations imply correlations of moderate magnitude among measures of the three components. A number of attempts have been made over the years to confirm the discriminant validity of measures designed to tap the different components (Bagozzi, 1978; Bagozzi and Burnkrant, 1979; Breckler, 1984; Kothandapani, 1971; Ostrom, 1969; Widaman, 1985). Depending on the method used and the assumptions made, the data have variously been interpreted either as supporting a tripartite model or a single-factor model [see the exchange between Dillon and

Kumar (1985) and Bagozzi and Burnkrant (1985)]. The major issue seems to revolve around whether differences between measures of the cognitive, affective, and conative components are to be inter- preted as due to differences in the procedures (scales) used to assess them (i.e. as theoretically uninteresting method variance) or as due to true differences between conceptually independent components. Generally speaking, however, most of the data reported in the literature is quite consistent with the hierarchical model in that a single factor is found to account for much of the variance in attitudinal responses, and the correlations among measures of the three components, although leaving room for some unique variance, are typically of considerable magnitude.

Perhaps the strongest evidence for the discriminant validity of measures assessing cognition, affect, and conation was reported by Breckler (1984). Yet, this study also demonstrates considerable commonality among the components. College students were asked to complete a questionnaire containing measures of cognition, affect, and conation while confronted with a caged, live snake. Agreement or disagreement with such statements as, "Snakes control the rodent population" and "Snakes will attack anything that moves," as well as ratings of snakes on scales labeled *kind–cruel, clean–dirty*, etc., were used to assess the cognitive component. A measure of the affective component was based on responses, in the presence of a snake, to such statements as "I feel anxious" and "I feel happy," as well as self-ratings of mood: carefree, elated, pleased, tense, fearful, sad, and so forth. Finally, a measure of each respondent's heart rate in the presence of the snake was also available. To assess the conative component, the investigator obtained responses to such statements as, "I scream whenever I see a snake" and "I like to handle snakes." In addition, the participants' willingness to interact with the snake in various ways was observed, and they were asked to rate how closely they would be willing to approach each of 12 snakes shown in color slides. Statistical analyses showed that the three types of responses could indeed be viewed as representing three different factors. At the same time, however, the correlations among the factors were of considerable magnitude. The cognition–affect correlation was 0.38, the affect–conation correlation was 0.50, and the correlation between cognition and conation was 0.70.

The hierarchical model of attitude, then, offers the following account of the way in which attitudes affect behavior. The actual or symbolic presence of an object elicits a generally favorable or unfavorable evaluative reaction, the attitude toward the object. This attitude, in turn, predisposes cognitive, affective, and conative responses to the object, responses whose evaluative tone is consistent with the overall attitude. It follows that individuals with positive attitudes toward, say, the medical profession should exhibit various favorable responses with respect to hospitals, doctors, nurses, etc., whereas individuals with negative attitudes toward the medical profession should exhibit unfavorable responses toward these objects.

## Summary and conclusions

This chapter showed that attitudes and personality traits are latent, hypothetical dispositions that are inferred from a variety of observable responses. Information about an individual's responses can be provided by the individual in the form of self-reports, it can be collected from friends or acquaintances, and it can be based on direct observation. Personality research has revealed five general response tendencies that represent robust personality characteristics: sociability, agreeableness, conscientiousness, emotional stability, and culturedness. In the attitude domain it is customary to distinguish between verbal or nonverbal responses that represent beliefs, feelings, and action tendencies. Some theorists have argued that these response classes reflect three separate and qualitatively distinct components of attitude: cognition, affect, and conation. A hierarchical model appears consistent with the results of empirical research. It encompasses evaluative attitude at the highest level, cognition, affect, and conation at an intermediate level, and specific beliefs, feelings, and action tendencies at the lowest level. Attitudes and personality traits are thus assumed to predispose overt behavior relevant to the trait or attitude under consideration.

## Notes

1. Several assumptions have to be met for the formula to hold, among them that inter-item correlations remain stable and that the new items have the same level of reliability as the original items on the scale.
2. It is also possible to use external criteria, such as the ability of each item to discriminate between groups known to differ in their attitudes or

personality traits, or their ability to predict attitude or personality scores obtained by other means.
3. Especially in personality assessment, a procedure known as factor analysis is often employed to identify items that reflect a given trait. The items thus selected also meet the criterion of internal consistency.

## Suggestions for further readings

1. Campbell, D. T. (1963). Social attitudes and other acquired behavioral dispositions. In S. Koch (Ed.), *Psychology: A study of a science*, Vol. 6, pp. 94–172. New York: McGraw-Hill. This chapter is a very thoughtful analysis of dispositional concepts, including traits and attitudes. Difficult but rewarding reading for the serious student.
2. Edwards, A. L. (1957). *Techniques of attitude scale construction*. New York: Appleton-Century-Crofts. A practical guide to various attitude scaling methods. Chapter 6 on the method of summated ratings (Likert scale) is of particular relevance.
3. Kleinmuntz, B. (1967). *Personality measurement: An introduction*. Homewood, IL: Dorsey. A basic introduction to personality assessment, this book reviews self-report as well as alternative measurement procedures.

The only completely consistent people are the dead.
*Aldous Huxley*

Dispositional explanation of human behavior presupposes a degree of coherence among thoughts, feelings, and actions. If people's reactions toward a given target were completely inconsistent across time and context, we could not attribute them to such stable underlying dispositions as attitudes or personality traits. In this chapter we examine consistency in human affairs, first from a theoretical point of view and then in the light of empirical research.

The historical and largely artificial boundaries between personality and social psychology have resulted in divergent research traditions that have tended to obscure the conceptual similarities and common vicissitudes of the trait and attitude concepts (Ajzen, 1982, 1987; Blass, 1984; Sherman and Fazio, 1983). As we saw in Chapter 1, personality traits and attitudes are typically conceived of as relatively enduring dispositions that exert pervasive influence on a broad range of behaviors. Both concepts gained wide popularity in the 1930s with the development of reliable psychometric techniques for their assessment, followed by a veritable avalanche of basic and applied research. For almost three decades the explanatory values and practical utilities of attitudes and traits went virtually unchallenged. Personality psychologists devoted considerable effort to the description of personality structures in terms of multidimensional trait configurations (e.g. Cattell, 1946; Eysenck, 1953; Jackson, 1967) while social psychologists – in addition to collecting descriptive data regarding attitudes toward various social issues – attended to the structure of attitudes in terms of their cognitive, affective and conative components (see Abelson *et al.*, 1968) and to effective strategies of persuasion and attitude change (see McGuire, 1985; Petty and Cacioppo, 1981, 1986). At the same time the new techniques and insights were applied to personnel selection, product design and promotion, political behavior, family planning, and a host of other more or less worthy causes. Traits and attitudes seemed assured of a central, lasting role in the prediction and explanation of human behavior.

To be sure, confidence in the trait and attitude concepts was not universal, but the occasional publication of cautionary notes or negative research findings went largely unnoticed. By the 1960s, however, doubts were being voiced with increasing frequency (see, e.g. DeFleur and Westie, 1958; Deutscher, 1966; McGuire, 1969; Peterson, 1968; Vernon, 1964). Much of the concern was related to the question of consistency.

## Psychological foundations of consistency

Consistency and regularity in the physical world are taken for granted. They permit us to make order and coherence out of the multitude of events that impinge on our senses every day. Night follows day and one season consistently follows another. Clouds produce rain, objects fall to the ground, lights throw shadows. Doors open when they are pushed or pulled and chairs generally support our weight. In the physical world the "laws of nature" generate consistency. Human thoughts and feelings, however, are not physical events. They are flexible and modifiable, not compelled by physical forces but obeying laws of their own. Why should they display consistency with each other or with observable behavior? Some theorists would claim that consistency in human behavior is more apparent than real: that we attribute to ourselves attitudes, motives, and personality traits consistent with our actions (e.g. Bem, 1965); that consistency is in the eye of the beholder rather than in observed behavior (e.g. Mischel, 1969; Nisbett and Ross, 1980; Shweder, 1975); that we express attitudes and values consistent with our actions in an effort to make a favorable impression on others (e.g. Tedeschi et al., 1971). Most theorists, however, maintain the position that consistency is a fundamental property of human thoughts, feelings, and actions. Divergence between theorists occurs mainly as a result of different interpretations that are given to observed consistencies.

*Preference for consistency*

Heider (1944, 1958) was perhaps the first social psychologist to propose a theoretical model based on an assumed preference for consistency over inconsistency. According to Heider's balance theory, people's beliefs and attitudes tend toward a state of balance or consistency: we tend to like people who agree with us, to associate positive properties with objects or people we value, to attribute negative motives to people we despise, to help people we admire, and so on. In balanced configurations of this kind, the elements of the situation fit together harmoniously; there is no stress to bring about change. However, when the configuration is imbalanced (e.g. a person we like commits a crime), tension is created which gives rise to action or cognitive reorganization designed to bring about a balanced state of affairs.

Basing his ideas largely on Heider's balance theory, Festinger (1957) examined the effects of inconsistency among cognitive elements, i.e. among beliefs or items of knowledge concerning the environment, oneself, or one's behavior. In Festinger's theory of cognitive dissonance, inconsistency between two beliefs exists when holding one belief conflicts with holding the other. For example, the belief that another person is ugly is dissonant with the knowledge that the person in question has won a beauty contest, just as buying a Porsche is dissonant with the belief that the car is overpriced. Inconsistency between cognitive elements is assumed to give rise to dissonance, a psychologically unpleasant state that motivates the individual to change one or more cognitive elements in an attempt to eliminate or reduce the magnitude of the existing dissonance. Thus, when people's overt actions conflict with their private attitudes or values, they are expected to try to reduce the resulting dissonance either by modifying their behaviors or by changing their attitudes.

It can be seen that the theories of balance and dissonance assume a motivation for people to maintain consistency among their beliefs, feelings, and actions. This motivation, however, is not considered to be a compelling force; rather, it resembles a preference or tendency of the cognitive system. As Zajonc (1968, p. 341) pointed out with respect to balance theory,

> the dynamic principle of change proposed by Heider does not involve psychological forces of overwhelming strength. They are more akin to *preferences* than to driving forces. There is no

anxiety when structures are imbalanced; imbalanced states are not noxious; a compelling need to strive for balance is not assumed.

## Functional consistency

Many theorists go beyond preferences to propose that consistency fulfills important needs in a person's life. Common to the different views is the assumption that maintenance of consistency in beliefs, feelings, and actions is essential for a person's effective functioning in the world.

### Need for effective action

It has been argued that consistency between one's beliefs and feelings with respect to an object makes it possible to develop a stable, action-directed orientation toward the object (Rosenberg, 1965). Consider, for example, a voter who is favorably disposed toward the Labour Party but who believes that the party's candidate for Prime Minister is unqualified for the office. This inconsistency makes it difficult for the voter to choose a course of action in the election. If, however, he could convince himself that the candidate is, after all, qualified to become Prime Minister, that is, if his belief about the candidate were to become consistent with his attitude toward the candidate's party, then the voting decision would be easy to make.

We may learn the need for consistency by repeatedly experiencing that we can act more effectively when beliefs and feelings are consistent than when they are inconsistent. In this fashion, we are assumed to develop a need to maintain consistency between the affective and cognitive components of our attitudes (Rosenberg, 1956, 1960). In Rosenberg's theory, the affective component of attitude is the overall positive or negative response to an object, while the cognitive component is made up of beliefs about the potentialities of the attitude object for attaining or blocking the realization of valued states. The assumption of affective–cognitive consistency implies that the more a given object is viewed as instrumental to obtaining positively valued goals and to blocking negative valued events, the more favorable will be the person's affect toward the object. For example, people should have positive feelings toward racial integration if they believe that integration enriches one's social life, reduces interracial conflict, improves educational opportunities, and so on, all favorably valued goals. By way of contrast, negative affect should accompany expectations to the effect that racial integration will produce such unfavorable outcomes as lower property values, interracial conflict, a deterioration in the quality of education, and so forth. Inconsistency is observed when people with positive feelings toward an object believe that it hinders attainment of valued goals and promotes attainment of negatively valued outcomes; or when people with negative feelings toward the object expect it to help them attain positively valued goals and to prevent the occurrence of negatively valued events. When cognition and affect are at odds, the need for consistency is assumed to activate processes that spawn changes in beliefs or feelings and thereby bring the attitude's cognitive and affective components in line with each other.

## Need for coherence

Some cognitive theorists postulate an overriding need for individuals to understand their worlds, and themselves within it, to be able to predict and control events (e.g. Epstein, 1980a; Kelly, 1955). Coherence and consistency are indispensable in our quest for understanding and prediction. Inconsistency between elements that comprise our intuitive theories of the world, be it inconsistency between beliefs, feelings, or actions, necessitates realignments to produce an internally consistent perspective. Once a coherent picture of some aspect of our world is established, it tends to be resistant to change. Of course, gradual shifts in our views occur all the time, but drastic changes must be resisted because they challenge fundamental assumptions and central values. In fact, challenges to our basic views of the world are held responsible for anxieties and other strong emotions that may produce abnormal behavior (cf. Epstein, 1983a).

Since the self is just another, albeit crucial, aspect of our worlds, the foregoing applies equally well to perceptions of ourselves. To act in ways that are inconsistent with our past behavior or with our important beliefs, attitudes, or values would undermine fundamental assumptions related to the self concept. Consider, for example, a woman who views herself as altruistic. If, on a given occasion, she refused to assist another individual in need of help, she might be able to rationalize her behavior, perhaps attributing it to circumstances, and maintain the image of herself as an altruist. However, repeated performance of trait-inconsistent behavior would make it increasingly difficult to preserve this image. Thus, our need to understand ourselves and to have a coherent picture of our own attitudes and personalities produces behavioral consistency.


## Inherent consistency

Some theoretical approaches assume, explicitly or implicitly, that human beings are inherently predisposed to think and act in consistent ways. Consistency, in these views, is not merely a preference, nor does it develop to serve other needs. Instead, it is an almost inevitable consequence of the way the human brain functions.


### Neuro-physiological dispositions

According to Allport (1935, p. 810), "An attitude is a mental and neural state of readiness, organized through experience, exerting a directive or dynamic influence upon the individual's response to all objects and situations with which it is related." In a similar fashion, Allport (1937, 1961) also speculated about the neurological base of personality traits. Although he had little evidence for it and did not make it a central feature of his theorizing, Allport seemed to assume that the basis for consistency in our thoughts and actions would ultimately be found in neurological mechanisms of the brain.

By way of comparison, Eysenck's (1947, 1967) theory of personality is a much more explicit attempt to tie behavioral consistencies to neuro-physiological processes. In his theory, traits – representing consistencies of behavior over time – are organized into constellations or syndromes, called personality types. Empirical investigations led Eysenck to conclude that personalities of the normal population consist of a small number of types which can be described in terms of two broad trait dimensions: extraversion, the extent to which a person is outgoing or reclusive, and neuroticism, the tendency to be excessively emotional and to respond with anxiety to stressful situations. An individual's personality type is thus defined in part by its degree of extraversion and neuroticism.[1]

Extraversion–introversion is assumed to reflect the balance between excitatory potentials and inhibitory potentials in the cerebral cortex (Eysenck, 1967). Specifically, the balance of these two potentials is said to be in favor of excitation for extraverted individuals and in favor of inhibition for introverted individuals. As to neuroticism, Eysenck proposed that it is related to the functioning of the brain's hypothalamus. A high level of neuroticism is assumed to be associated with a low threshold for excitation of the hypothalamus, i.e. the hypothalamus of relatively neurotic individuals is more easily stimulated to an excessive degree. In short, according to Eysenck's theory, characteristic brain processes predispose people to behave in a consistently extraverted or introverted manner, and to exhibit a high or low degree of emotionality in their reactions to stress.

Intuitively, it seems reasonable to expect that at least some behavioral dispositions have a strong neurophysiological component. Excitability in the personality domain and attitudes toward such emotionally arousing stimuli as snakes or spiders are perhaps good examples. Most traits and attitudes, however, are much less likely to be tied to specific neurophysiological mechanisms, and to be more a function of socialization and learning. Dependability, preferences for certain fashions, and political attitudes are a few examples that come readily to mind. Although they tend to exhibit some degree of stability over time, behavioral dispositions of this kind are much more likely to change in response to experience than are dispositions that have their base in neurophysiological processes of the brain.

## Logical consistency

Some theorists have suggested that we are inherently consistent in our responses because of the way we process information and make decisions. For example, McGuire (1960a, 1960b) proposed a model of logical consistency that combines formal logic and statistical probability theory. The model deals with the situation in which a conclusion follows logically from two related premises, i.e. with logical syllogisms. To illustrate, the premises, "All citizens of countries that are members of the European Economic Community are permitted to reside and work in Britain" and "Pierre B. is a citizen of a member country" logically imply that Pierre B. is permitted to reside and work in Britain. In his research, McGuire found that, by and large, people display a fair amount of logical consistency in their beliefs, although one can also observe certain biases and discrepancies. Perhaps more important, after reviewing their beliefs, people tend to change some of them in the direction of increased logical consistency, a phenomenon McGuire (1960b) termed the "Socratic effect." This finding indicates that people can recognize logical inconsistencies among the beliefs they hold and that this recognition is sufficient to bring about increased consistency without any added outside pressure.

The assumption that people think and act in more or less logical ways is also embedded in Fishbein and Ajzen's (1975; Ajzen and Fishbein, 1980) theory of reasoned action. Rather than treating cognition, affect, and conation as three components of attitude, Fishbein and Ajzen prefer to treat these three types of response tendencies as independent constructs termed, respectively, belief, attitude, and intention. According to the theory of reasoned action, attitudes follow reasonably from the beliefs people hold about the object of the attitude, just as intentions and actions follow reasonably from attitudes.

Consider first how the formation of beliefs may lead reasonably to the development of attitudes that are consistent with those beliefs. Generally speaking, we form beliefs about an object by associating it with certain attributes, i.e. with other objects, characteristics, or events. Thus, perhaps as a result of watching a television program, we may come to believe that the former military government of Argentina (the object) was corrupt, abducted innocent civilians, and mismanaged the economy (attributes). Since the attributes that come to be linked to the object are already valued positively or negatively, we automatically and simultaneously acquire an attitude toward the object. In this fashion, we learn to like objects we believe have largely desirable characteristics, and we form unfavorable attitudes toward objects we associate with mostly undesirable characteristics. Specifically, the subjective value of each attribute contributes to the attitude in direct proportion to the strength of the belief, i.e. the subjective probability that the object has the attribute in question. The way in which beliefs combine to produce an attitude is shown in Equation 2.1.

$$A \propto \Sigma b_i e_i \qquad (2.1)$$

As can be seen, the strength of each belief ($b$) is multiplied by the subjective evaluation ($e$) of the belief's attribute and the resulting products are summed. A person's attitude is expected to be directly proportional ($\propto$) to this summative belief index.

It may be noted that this expectancy-value model of attitude is structurally similar to Rosenberg's (1956) theory of affective–cognitive consistency. However, in contrast to Rosenberg's theory, the model described here does not make the assumption that people have a *need* for consistency; instead, the connection between beliefs and attitudes is construed in terms of reasonable information processing. In addition, whereas an assumed need for affective–cognitive consistency implies mutual influence between the two types of responses, the present model is concerned mainly with the unidirectional effects of beliefs on attitudes.

In the course of our lives we acquire many different beliefs about a variety of objects, actions, and events. These beliefs may be formed as a result of direct observation, they may be self-generated by way of inference processes, or they may be formed indirectly by accepting information from such outside sources as friends, television, newspapers, books, and so on. Some beliefs may persist over time, others may weaken or disappear, and new beliefs may be formed. People can hold a great many beliefs about any given object, but they can attend to only a relatively small number, perhaps eight or nine, at any given moment (see Miller, 1956). It is these *salient* beliefs that are the immediate determinants of a person's attitude (Fishbein, 1963; Fishbein and Ajzen, 1975).

Just as attitudes are said to flow reasonably and spontaneously from beliefs, so are intentions and actions seen to follow reasonably from attitudes. Ajzen and Fishbein's theory of reasoned action postulates that, as a general rule, we intend to behave in favorable ways with respect to things and people we like and to display unfavorable behaviors toward things and people we dislike. And, barring unforeseen events, we translate our plans into actions. In short, the theory of reasoned action posits a causal sequence of events in which actions with respect to an object follow directly from behavioral intentions, the intentions are evaluatively consistent with the attitude toward the object, and this attitude derives reasonably from salient beliefs about the object. A more detailed discussion and elaboration of the links postulated by the theory of reasoned action is presented in Chapter 6.

## Empirical evidence

Clearly, there are many good reasons for expecting people to display consistency in their thoughts, feelings, and actions. Among them are the desire to project a favorable image of the self, perceptual and motivational preferences for consistent configurations of elements related to the self, and satisfaction of various needs served by consistency. Further, some of these tendencies and needs may be related to inherent biologically based dispositions toward consistency. One might presume, in the light of these considerations, that it would be easy to demonstrate consistency in people's responses to an object or situation, consistency between the way they think and feel and the way they act.

Casual observation indeed appears to support the presence of consistency in human affairs. We have the impression that some of our acquaintances are generally friendly and outgoing, while others are more introverted and shy; that some people are honest to a fault, while others cannot be trusted; that some of our coworkers behave in a consistently reliable manner, while others are annoyingly unreliable. By the same token, it would appear that we generally associate with people we like, that we eat foods we consider tasty and nutritious, that we support policies we consider desirable, and that we generally behave in accordance with our attitudes. We thus turn to an examination of some empirical research in personality and social psychology that has dealt with the question of consistency.

*Behavioral consistency*

An important implication of the dispositional view of human behavior is that general response tendencies should manifest themselves across a variety of actions and situations. An individual who has a disposition to act impulsively might be expected not only to leave the scene of a traffic accident but also to purchase even relatively expensive items on the spur of the moment, to strike another person when insulted or angry, to eat at irregular intervals, to quit a job without warning, and so on. Conversely, a person who displays a lack of impulsivity in one situation should also act in a deliberate manner in other situations. Or, to take another example, if returning books on time to the library is evidence of a stable disposition, say, conscientiousness, then it should follow that people who perform this behavior will also act conscientiously in other ways. They might be expected to remember birthdays of family members and friends, to prepare assignments diligently, to take good care of their possessions, and so forth. The dispositional view thus implies *behavioral consistency*, that is, consistency across different behaviors, performed in different situations, so long as the behaviors in question are all instances of the same underlying disposition. In fact, Campbell (1963) made it clear that behavioral dispositions are evidenced by, and can only be inferred from, consistency in responses. It follows that without response consistency we have no evidence for the existence of stable traits or attitudes.

This is not to say, however, that behavioral consistency is always to be expected. Inconsistency of behavior from one occasion to another can be introduced by factors related to the person performing the behavior, that is, personal factors other than the attitude or personality trait of interest; by factors related to the situation in which the behavior is performed (the context, the target at which the behavior is directed, etc.); and by factors related to the action selected to represent the behavioral domain. Thus, an individual with a positive attitude toward the blind may on one occasion help a blind person across the street and on another occasion pass without offering help. The difference in behavior could be due to differences in mood or attentiveness on the two occasions, to differences in the age of the blind person or the amount of traffic on the road, or to other personal or contextual factors. Another type of inconsistency across occasions can be observed when the individual with a positive attitude toward the blind helps a blind person across the street on one occasion, but on another occasion refuses to assist a blind person in filling out an application form. Here, the difference in behavior can be due not only to differences in personal or situational factors on the two occasions, but also to differences between the two particular actions chosen to represent the behavioral domain of helping the blind.

Empirical research has uncovered little consistency between single actions, even if both actions are taken from the same behavioral domain. Evidence for behavioral inconsistency was presented as early as 1928 by Hartshorne and May who showed, for example, that dishonesty of a specific kind in a given context (e.g. copying from another student's test paper) was virtually unrelated to dishonesty of a different kind in a different context (e.g. telling a lie outside the classroom). LaPiere's (1934) well-known investigation of racial discrimination can also be seen as supporting the same argument. In the early 1930s, LaPiere accompanied a young Chinese couple in their travels through the United States. Calling on 251 restaurants, hotels, and other establishments, they were refused service only once. About 6 months later, LaPiere sent a letter to each establishment they had visited, asking the following question: "Will you accept members of the Chinese race as guests in your establishment?" Of the 128 establishments that replied, over 90% answered, "No." One single action: accepting a Chinese couple as guests in a restaurant or hotel, was found to be inconsistent with another single action: refusal to accept Chinese guests expressed in response to a written inquiry. Findings of this kind are of course hardly surprising if we recall that any single response tends to be highly unreliable. That is, inconsistency between different actions may be due, at least in part, to unreliability of measurement (see Epstein, 1979, 1980b, 1983b).

Of greater interest, therefore, is the relation between two single actions when each is reliably assessed. This can be achieved by summing observations of each action across occasions. An early indication that behavioral consistency is low even under such favorable conditions was provided by Dudycha (1936) who reported correlations among several summative measures of behavior related to punctuality: time of arrival at 8 a.m. classes, at college commons, at appointments, at extracurricular activities, at vesper services, and at entertainments. A correlation of moderate magnitude ($r = 0.44$) was observed between punctuality at commons and at entertainments, but the other correlations were much lower – the average correlation was 0.19.

An example in the attitudinal domain is provided by Minard's (1952) study of race relations among black and white coal miners. Through interviews and observations, Minard discovered a general pattern of integration in the mines but widespread segregation in the community. Black and white miners tended to interact freely and on good terms in the mines, but little contact was maintained or permitted after working hours. Specifically, about 60% of the white miners displayed this inconsistent pattern of behavior, while approximately 20% discriminated in both settings and another 20% discriminated in neither.

More recent research has also provided little evidence in support of behavioral consistency. For example, Funder et al. (1983) obtained two scaled resistance-to-temptation measures in children: resisting approach to a present and resisting attractive but "forbidden" toys. Although the scales' reliabilities were not reported, each was based on more than a single observation and was thus likely to have had at least some degree of reliability. The correlation between them, however, was only 0.20. Similarly, even after summing over several behavioral self-reports, Epstein (1979, Study 3) found only very low and mostly nonsignificant correlations between individual behaviors seemingly tapping the same underlying disposition. Thus, the correlation between the number of telephone calls made over a period of time and the number of letters written in the same time interval was 0.33, and the correlation between the number of absences from class and the number of papers not submitted was below 0.30 – neither correlation was statistically significant. In a systematic re-examination of behavioral consistency with reliable measures, Mischel and Peake (1982a, 1982b) presented data in the domain of conscientiousness among college students. Nineteen different action tendencies were observed on repeated occasions, including class attendance, punctuality in handing in assignments, thoroughness of notes taken, and neatness of personal appearance. The average correlation among these different kinds of actions representing conscientiousness was a mere 0.13.

In short, empirical research has shown very little support for consistency between different behaviors presumed to reflect the same underlying disposition. We will return to the problem of behavioral consistency and how it might be increased in Chapter 3. At this point, we must consider one additional source of evidence for inconsistency, namely, research on the relation between global measures of attitudes or personality traits and particular behaviors.


*Predictive validity*

In addition to the failure of empirical research to confirm behavioral consistency, the problem of inconsistency also arose in a different sense, namely, in the sense of *predictive validity*. Defined as relatively enduring response dispositions, attitudes and personality traits are naturally assumed to direct, and in some way determine, social action. Thus, a hostile personality disposition should produce aggressive behavior, and liberal or conservative attitudes should result in corresponding political actions. As we saw in Chapter 1, attitudes and traits are typically inferred from verbal responses to questionnaire items. If these attitude and personality scales indeed assess enduring response dispositions, they should predict how an individual will actually behave in a concrete situation. A person who expresses a favorable attitude toward religion on a questionnaire might be expected to attend Sunday worship services, pray before meals, participate in bible classes, watch religious television programs, and so forth. Conversely, nonreligious individuals, as assessed by means of an attitude scale, might not perform any of these behaviors, although they might engage in premarital sex, disobey their parents, and do other things a religious person would be expected to avoid.

Before continuing the discussion of predictive validity, it is important to realize that attitudes and personality traits can express themselves, and can therefore be inferred from verbal as well as nonverbal responses. This point is often misunderstood. Many investigators assume that verbal responses reflect a person's attitude or personality trait, whereas nonverbal ("overt") actions are measures of behavior. In point of fact, however, both verbal and nonverbal responses are observable behaviors. Neither is more or less a measure of attitude or personality than the other; both types of behavior can reflect the same underlying disposition (cf. Roth and Upmeyer, 1985; Upmeyer, 1981). Moreover, the validity of overt behaviors as indicators of a latent disposition cannot be taken for granted, any more so than can the validity of verbal responses to questionnaire items. Both types of behavior must be submitted to standard scaling procedures, and only some responses – verbal or nonverbal – will be found adequate for the assessment of a given attitude or personality trait (cf. Ajzen and Fishbein, 1980; Jackson and Paunonen, 1985). Some time ago, Merton (1940, p. 20) made the same point very succinctly:

> The metaphysical assumption is tacitly introduced that in one sense or another overt behavior is "more real" than verbal behavior. This assumption is both unwarranted and scientifically meaningless. . . . It should not be forgotten that overt actions may deceive; that they, just as "derivations" or "speech reactions" may be deliberately designed to disguise or to conceal private attitudes.

Strictly speaking, therefore, most tests of the "attitude–behavior" or "trait–behavior" relation are better conceptualized as tests of the relation between verbal and nonverbal indicators of the same underlying disposition. However, for the sake of simplicity, and in line with common practice, we will continue to refer to attitude–behavior and trait–behavior relations.

The research on behavioral consistency reviewed earlier showed little relation between two or more actions that were assumed to reflect the same underlying disposition. The approach discussed in the present section attempts to predict performance or nonperformance of a given behavior, or a narrow range of behaviors, from global dispositional measures, typically obtained by means of a questionnaire.

## Global attitudes and specific actions

General attitudes have been assessed with respect to a variety of targets, including organizations and institutions (the church, public housing, student government, one's job or employer), minority groups (Blacks, Jews, Catholics), and particular individuals with whom one might interact (a Black person, a fellow student). Attitudes of this kind are then often used to predict one or more specific acts directed at the attitude object.

A good example is the experiment reported by Himmelstein and Moore (1963). A sample of white male college students first completed a scale assessing attitudes toward Blacks and, some time later, reported for a psychology experiment. Upon arrival, the participant found another student (a confederate), either Black or white, already seated in the room. While they were waiting for the experiment to begin, a (white) confederate entered the room holding in his hand a petition to extend the university's library hours on Saturday nights. The Black or white confederate either signed or refused to sign the petition and, following this manipulation, the naive participant was asked to sign. His conformity or lack of conformity with the response of the confederate served as the measure of behavior. The data revealed a nonsignificant correlation between general attitudes toward Blacks and conformity with the Black confederate.

In a review of attitude–behavior research, Ajzen and Fishbein (1977) discovered many studies of this kind: of the 109 investigations reviewed, 54 assessed general attitudes in attempts to predict specific actions. Of these studies, 25 obtained nonsignificant results and the remainder rarely showed correlations in excess of 0.40.

## Global personality traits and specific actions

Examination of the personality literature reveals a comparable pattern of results: correlations between global personality characteristics and narrowly defined behaviors relevant to the trait in question are often nonsignificant and rarely exceed the 0.30 level. In fact, the search for explanations of narrowly defined behaviors in terms of global personality traits has, as a general rule, turned out to be a frustrating experience (cf. Mischel, 1984; Mischel and Peake, 1982a), and many an investigator has given up in despair.

One example is provided by the large number of investigations that have attempted to identify unique personality characteristics of group leaders. To be sure, leadership behavior is not a single act. It is usually assessed by observing the amount of influence a person exerts in a group, by retrospective judgments of group members, or by nominations for leadership. A measure of leadership thus encompasses a range of different behaviors reflecting influence on others in a group setting. Nevertheless, the behaviors involved are much narrower in scope than the broad personality characteristics usually considered in this context, which include such traits as dominance, responsibility, interpersonal sensitivity, need for power, self-esteem, etc. In an extensive review of the literature, Mann (1959) summarized obtained relations between measures of leadership and various personality characteristics. Among his summary results were the following: the median correlation of leadership with adjustment across different investigations was about 0.25; with extra-introversion it was about 0.15; and no significant correlations were reported with masculinity–femininity. In a more recent review of the available research in this area, Gibb (1969, p. 227) concluded that ". . . numerous studies of the personalities of leaders have failed to find any consistent pattern of traits which characterize leaders."

Another area of research demonstrating the low predictive validity of personality characteristics has to do with the everyday behavior of driving an automobile. Numerous studies have attempted to relate the personality traits of drivers to errors made while driving, to traffic violations, and to involvement in traffic accidents. In their review of this research, Knapper and Cropley (1981) stated that the best predictors of good or poor driving tend to be relatively superficial factors, such as years of driving experience and a history of past court appearances. However, "Disappointingly, this kind of research has failed to yield any definite conclusions about personality syndromes underlying good or bad driving" (p. 197).

Overweight and control of body weight is another area of research in which the search for personality correlates of narrowly defined behaviors has proved rather futile.[2] Although it is well known that there are great individual differences in people's ability to control their body weight,

> Prediction of individual differences in weight loss has not at all been successful. Clinical intuition, MMPI, MPI, weight prior to treatment, general anxiety, situation specific anxiety, PAS,

EPQ, I-E scale, body image measures, and the 16 PF question-naire have all failed to predict success in treatment (Hall and Hall, 1974, p. 362).[3]

Looking more generally at the traits of obese individuals, Leon and Roth (1977) summarized their review of the research literature as follows: "The evidence strongly suggests that there are very few personality characteristics that obese persons share that can be considered causative in the development of obesity" (p. 136).

Other illustrations of the same phenomenon abound, but the main point to be made is clear: research in diverse domains paints a discouraging picture of our ability to predict specific or narrowly defined behaviors from the knowledge of people's general personality characteristics.

## Implications

To summarize briefly, years of research failed to demonstrate impressive consistency among different behavioral manifestations of the same disposition. By the late 1960s it had become evident that in contrast to casual observation, empirical research failed to provide strong support for behavioral consistency or predictive validity of traits and attitudes. People were found neither to behave consistently across situations, nor to act in accordance with their measured attitudes and personality traits. The accumulation of research findings of this kind undermined confidence in the trait approach among personality psychologists and cast doubts on the practices of social psychologists who relied on the attitude concept in their attempts to predict and explain human behavior.

The alarm in the domain of personality psychology was sounded by Mischel (1968) who, after reviewing the literature, reached the following conclusions:

> . . . it is evident that the behaviors which are often construed as stable personality trait indicators actually are highly specific and depend on the details of the evoking situations and the response mode employed to measure them (p. 37).

> With the possible exception of intelligence, highly generalized behavioral consistencies have not been demonstrated, and the concept of personality traits as broad response predispositions is thus untenable (p. 146).

The greatest challenge to the utility of the attitude concept was posed by Wicker's (1969) review of the literature in which he summarized,

> Taken as a whole, these studies suggest that it is considerably more likely that attitudes will be unrelated or only slightly related to overt behaviors than that attitudes will be closely related to actions. Product–moment correlation coefficients relating the two kinds of responses are rarely above .30, and often are near zero (p. 65).

And, like Mischel in the personality domain, Wicker concluded:

> The present review provides little evidence to support the postulated existence of stable, underlying attitudes within the individual which influence both his verbal expressions and his actions (p. 75).

There is also an interesting parallel between Wicker's conclusion regarding the magnitude of typical attitude–behavior correlations and Mischel's (1968) view with respect to the predictive validity of personality traits. Mischel coined the term "personality coefficient" to describe

> . . . the correlation between .20 and .30 which is found persistently when virtually any personality dimension inferred from a questionnaire is related to almost any conceivable external criterion involving responses sampled in a *different* medium – that is, not by another questionnaire (p. 78).

Thus, by the end of the 1960s, personality and social psychologists had lost their faith in the trait and attitude concepts, and had concluded that only a very small proportion of behavioral variance could be explained by reference to these dispositions.

### Summary and conclusions

This chapter reviewed a variety of theoretical approaches that assume consistency in people's beliefs, feelings and actions and it presented some preliminary evidence that seems to contradict this assumption. In theory, consistency in human affairs is preferred because of its perceptual simplicity or because inconsistency is psychologically uncomfortable; it serves the needs for coherence and effective action;

and it is inherent in human nature as a result of neurophysiological processes and the capacity for logical reasoning. Yet, despite the many good reasons why people should exhibit consistency, empirical research has uncovered considerable inconsistency of behavior across situations and between verbal and nonverbal measures of a disposition.

Lack of behavioral consistency is an embarrassing problem for personality and social psychologists. A person's behavior on one occasion suggests a friendly disposition and on another an unfriendly disposition, one day it implies that the person opposes nuclear power but on another that he favors it. In a similar fashion, carefully constructed measures of friendliness, honesty, or attitudes toward nuclear power are unrelated to observed behavior in specific contexts. Not only does such a lack of consistency call into question the very notions of attitudes and personality traits as stable response dispositions, it also undermines our understanding of personality functioning, it challenges our theories of attitude structure and change, and it denies the possibility of effective social interaction.

The remainder of this book is devoted to discussions of various attempts that have been made to cope with the consistency dilemma. We shall see that initial expectations for the predictive validity of trait and attitude measures may have been unduly optimistic and perhaps a bit naive, and that we now have a much better understanding of the complexities involved. We shall also see that considerable progress has been made toward a resolution of the consistency dilemma and that the trait and attitude concepts have gradually regained their central positions in personality and social psychology.

## Notes

1. Eysenck's theory includes two other major personality dimensions: intelligence and, mainly in the case of clinical populations, psychoticism.
2. As in the case of leadership, reducing and maintaining weight involve a set of behaviors (dieting, exercising), not a single action (see Ajzen and Fishbein, 1980), but their range is much more narrowly defined than is the range of behaviors encompassed by the personality traits used to predict weight control.
3. The MMPI, MPI, PAS, EPQ, I-E scale, and 16 PF questionnaire are multi-item instruments designed to measure a variety of personality traits.

## Suggestions for further readings

1. Abelson, R. P., Aronson, E., McGuire, W. J., Newcomb, T. M., Rosenberg, M. J. and Tannenbaum, P. H. (Eds) (1968). *Theories of cognitive consistency: A sourcebook.* Chicago: Rand McNally. This book is a collection of articles that provide a thorough discussion of theoretical issues related to consistency in human affairs.
2. Wicker, A. W. (1969). Attitudes versus actions: The relationship of verbal and overt behavioral responses to attitude objects. *Journal of Social Issues,* **25**, 41–78. This article set the stage for the re-examination of the attitude–behavior relation. It presents a review of empirical papers showing little correspondence between verbal attitudes and overt actions.
3. Ajzen, I. and Fishbein, M. (1977). Attitude–behavior relations: A theoretical analysis and review of empirical research. *Psychological Bulletin,* **84**, 888–918. Providing a more recent review of the attitude–behavior literature, this article emphasizes the importance of compatibility between attitude and behavior measures.
4. Mischel, W. (1968). *Personality and assessment.* New York: Wiley. This influential book challenged the utility of the trait concept.
5. Epstein, S. (1979). The stability of behavior: I. On predicting most of the people much of the time. *Journal of Personality and Social Psychology,* **37**, 1097–1126. With this article, Epstein began his challenge of the critique to which personality traits had been submitted.

# 3 / THE PRINCIPLE OF AGGREGATION

Confusion is a word we have invented for an order which is not understood.

*Henry Miller*

On a foggy evening in February a man is driving his battered van along a narrow country road. He is returning home after a tiring day of work and a few drinks in a nearby pub. The road is winding, visibility is poor, and he is careful to keep within the posted speed limit. Suddenly, as if out of nowhere, a pedestrian is caught in the headlights. The driver's reaction is sluggish. He tries to avoid the man and applies the brakes, but it is too late. The van skids and the side of the vehicle strikes the man with a disconcerting thump. The driver is wide awake now. Within seconds he makes up his mind. He straightens the van and steps on the accelerator, leaving the scene of the accident and the victim to his fate.

A deplorable, but not unknown, instance of human behavior. How are we to explain the driver's failure to assist the man he has hurt? Certainly, a great many factors may be involved: fatigue at the end of a long day, the privacy of a deserted country road in evening fog, the influence of alcohol, fear of dealing with the police, of facing family and friends, a general reluctance to get involved in a messy, time-consuming, unpleasant affair. Every particular instance of human action is, in this way, determined by a unique set of factors. Any change in circumstances, be it ever so slight, might produce a different reaction. If the driver had possessed a greater sense of personal responsibility; if the accident had occurred on a well-traveled highway; if it had not been a foggy evening; if the driver had not been under the influence of alcohol; if he had not been so exhausted; if the victim had been a woman or a child; if the driver could have seen the victim's face; if any of these things had been true, the driver might have stopped his van and offered his help.

Many instances of human behavior are "overdetermined," in the sense that a multitude of factors combine to produce them. However, it is not the role of the psychologist to account for unique instances of human action. Detectives called to investigate the hit-and-run accident might try to reconstruct the exact circumstances, although they would probably be more interested in establishing the identity of the driver involved than in the reasons for his behavior. Perhaps it is the historian who is most concerned with unique events. An individual's behavior on a particular occasion can have momentous consequences, especially if the individual is in a position of power. To understand the unique combination of factors that led up to the behavior is to provide a possible explanation of the events that followed. But psychologists are not historians; they are rarely interested in an individual's action on any particular occasion. Instead, they are engaged in building a science of human behavior, in establishing the general laws of human action. Of concern to the psychologist, therefore, are *regularities* in behavior, consistent *patterns* of action, response *tendencies*. In line with this goal, attitudes and personality traits are concepts designed to capture the dispositional nature of human behavior.

In Chapter 2 we saw that enthusiasm for the trait and attitude concepts was followed, in the 1960s, by a period of disenchantment due mainly to failures of research to find evidence for consistency across behavior or for predictive validity of trait and attitude measures. Just as infatuation and disappointment with the trait and attitude concepts followed parallel lines, so did the proposed remedies for observed inconsistencies that emerged in the 1970s. One popular solution advanced by personality and social psychologists is aggregation of observations across actions and situations. In the present chapter we consider the principle of aggregation and examine empirical research of relevance to that principle.

### The logic of aggregation

Regularities, patterns, or tendencies cannot be discerned in single instances of behavior. Rather, to obtain a measure of a behavioral tendency, we must aggregate observations made on different occasions. When we compute the average behavioral tendency over repeated occasions, the influence of factors that vary from one occasion to another tends to "cancel out." Consider, for example, the act of engaging (or not engaging) in a conversation with a stranger. When observed on particular occasions, this behavior – like the behavior of the driver in the hit-and-run accident – is overdetermined. On one occasion an individual approached by a stranger stops to talk, but on another occasion he hurries past the stranger. A multitude of factors may account for the different reactions: mood states, the press of time, weather conditions, the stranger's appearance, and so on. Factors of this kind tend to intrude in a more or less random fashion. That is to say, they are not present consistently across occasions. The weather varies from one occasion to another, as does one's mood and time schedule, or the physical appearance of different strangers.

Repeated observations of the same action inevitably involve different contexts. Although it is possible in principle to conceive of observing a given behavior under identical conditions on two or more occasions, conditions are rarely if ever identical in practice. Given these rather arbitrary variations in the presence or absence of factors that could influence whether or not we engage in a conversation with a stranger, observation of the behavior on a single occasion is a poor measure of a person's "typical" reaction, i.e. of the general response tendency. By aggregating over different occasions, however, we eliminate the systematic impact of these arbitrary factors. Averaged over many different occasions, the number of times a person is seen engaging in a conversation with a stranger cannot be attributed to the weather, to temporary moods, or to competing demands on the person's time. Instead, the aggregate measure represents the influence of factors consistently present across different occasions, i.e. the disposition to perform the particular behavior in question. This idea is embedded in the Spearman-Brown prophecy formula described in Chapter 1, and its implications are usually well understood (see Mischel, 1968; Mischel and Peake, 1982a, 1982b) if not always heeded in empirical research (cf. Epstein, 1980b).

The same logic can be applied to behavioral dispositions that reflect general attitudes or personality traits. We have noted repeatedly that traits and attitudes, as usually defined, represent very broad behavioral dispositions. It stands to reason that such broad dispositions can be validly inferred only from equally broad sets of response tendencies. Consider again the disposition toward extraversion or introversion. Even when aggregated over a large number of occasions, talking to strangers is unrepresentative of a person's general disposition to be sociable. We mean much more by sociability than merely the tendency to engage in conversations with strangers. It also involves maintaining contacts with old friends, making new friends, going to parties, interacting with coworkers on the job, going to the movies with acquaintances, and 101 other ways of being outgoing or reclusive. Any single one of these response tendencies is influenced by factors that may be irrelevant for the others. Thus, going to parties is affected not only by one's sociability but perhaps also by the availability of babysitters on weekends, by involvement in such competing social activities on Saturday nights as playing cards or going bowling with friends, etc. Interacting with coworkers on the job, however, is unlikely to be affected by these kinds of factors. Instead, the variables that, besides sociability, may influence the tendency to interact with coworkers include perhaps the nature of one's job, encouragement or discouragement of inter- action by management, and so forth.

In short, general behavioral dispositions can be inferred by ap- plying the principle of aggregation to the varied types of specific response tendencies, thus eliminating the contaminating influence of variables other than the disposition of interest. In addition to aggregating repeated observations of a given action to obtain a high degree of consistency across occasions, it is possible to aggregate different actions in a given behavioral domain, observed on various occasions and in diverse contexts. Based on a representative set of responses, such a *multiple-act* index should serve as a valid indicator of the underlying disposition.

Our discussion of aggregation as a means of securing behavioral measures that are stable across occasions or that are representative of broad underlying dispositions is summarized in Table 3.1. The table's rows represent different behaviors and its columns represent observations on different occasions. Each cell in the table contains performance (or nonperformance) of a single behavior observed on a single occasion, i.e. a *single-act criterion* ($S_{11}, S_{12}, \ldots$). By aggregat- ing across the columns within a given row, we obtain, in the row margins, specific *behavioral tendencies*, i.e. tendencies to perform particular behaviors over time ($T_1$, $T_2$, $\ldots$). In a comparable fashion, we can aggregate rows within a given column and obtain *multiple-act criteria*, as shown in the column margins of Table 3.1 ($M_1, M_2, \ldots$). The different behaviors that enter into these measures are each observed on a single occasion. Finally, the best multiple-act measure of behavior is obtained when temporally stable action tendencies are aggregated. This multiple-act, repeated occasions

*Table 3.1*    Aggregation of behavior (after Fishbein and Ajzen, 1975)

| Behaviors | Occasions | | | | | Behavioral tendencies |
|---|---|---|---|---|---|---|
| | 1 | 2 | . . . | . . . | $n$ | |
| 1 | $S_{11}$ | $S_{12}$ | . . . | . . . | $S_{1n}$ | $T_1$ |
| 2 | . | | | | | $T_2$ |
| 3 | . | | | | | $T_3$ |
| 4 | . | | | | | $T_4$ |
| . | . | | | | | . |
| . | . | | | | | . |
| . | . | | | | | . |
| . | . | | | | | . |
| $m$ | $S_{m1}$ | $S_{m2}$ | . . . | . . . | $S_{mn}$ | $T_m$ |
| Multiple-act criteria | $M_1$ | $M_2$ | . . . | . . . | $M_n$ | Behavioral disposition |

criterion is the grand mean which, in Table 3.1, is shown as "behavioral disposition". It represents the aggregation of all cells in the table.

According to the principle of aggregation, neither single-act criteria nor the tendency to perform a specific behavior over time are representative of general traits or attitudes. Only multiple-act criteria are sufficiently general to reflect such broad underlying dispositions. It follows that only multiple-act indices of behavior can be expected to display consistency across situations and to correlate well with verbal measures of general traits and attitudes. By way of comparison, much of the negative research evidence reviewed in Chapter 2 was collected in studies that used tendencies to engage in single actions, or narrowly defined classes of actions, as their behavioral criteria. Behavioral consistency was usually examined by correlating one specific action tendency (e.g. returning books to the library on time) with another specific action tendency (e.g. being on time for appointments); and global measures of traits or attitudes (e.g. dominance, sociability, attitude toward Blacks or toward the church) were used to predict narrow action tendencies deemed relevant for the trait or directed at the attitude object (e.g. using birth control methods, writing letters, conforming with the petition-signing behavior of a Black individual). As shown above, the problem with this approach is that single behaviors are typically invalid or poor indicators of an underlying disposition. To claim evidence for inconsistency, the indicators found to be inconsistent with one another must each be based on an appropriate sample of responses from which the latent disposition can be validly inferred. Only when this condition is met can the lack of correspondence between observed behaviors be taken as evidence against the existence of a stable behavioral disposition.

## Consistency of behavioral aggregates

The question of behavioral consistency has to do with the relation between two behavioral manifestations of the same disposition. Since a single action on a particular occasion is often a poor indicator of the general behavioral tendency, we can at most expect rather low levels of consistency among single actions. Similarly, since single behavioral tendencies (even when aggregated over occasions) are generally unrepresentative of a general behavioral domain, they too cannot be expected to correlate well with each other. Both of these expectations are well borne out by empirical research (see Chapter 2). However, if the logic of aggregation can be applied to the problem of consistency, then two multiple-observation or multiple-act indices, each representative of the same behavioral tendency or disposition, should correlate highly with each other.

### Consistency across occasions

The empirical literature of recent years provides strong and persuasive evidence for the importance of aggregation to achieve stability of behavior across occasions. In one of his studies concerning this issue Epstein (1979, Study 4) asked college students to record, among other things, some of their behaviors on each day of a 14-day period. The behaviors recorded were the number of telephone calls made, the number of letters written, the number of social contacts initiated, the number of hours slept, and the number of hours studied. Consistency of behavior on any 2 days chosen at random was relatively low, ranging from a reliability coefficient of 0.26 for the number of telephone calls made to 0.63 for the number of social contacts initiated. Behavioral stability increased dramatically when the behavioral indices were aggregated across more than one observation. The comparison of average behavioral scores on the 7 odd days with average behavioral scores on the 7 even days produced correlations of 0.81 and 0.94 for the number of phone calls and number of social contacts, respectively. Clear evidence for stability of aggregate measures based on repeated observations has also been reported by Olweus (1979) in a review of research on aggressive behavior. Pooling data from a large number of longitudinal studies, the stability of aggregated aggression scores over two points in time was, on average, found to be 0.68.

Similar results can be found in the domain of conscientiousness. As mentioned in Chapter 2, Mischel and Peake (1982a, 1982b) obtained data concerning the repeated performance or nonperformance of 19 different behaviors related to conscientiousness, such as class attendance, punctuality, and thoroughness of note taking. Like Epstein, they found that even though stability of single observations was quite low (the average correlation between observations on two individual occasions was 0.29), it could be greatly increased (to 0.65 on average) by aggregating across observations.

## Cross-situational consistency

The demonstration that high behavioral stability can be established by aggregating observations across occasions is, however, not at the heart of the consistency debate, as Mischel (1983; Mischel and Peake, 1982a) has taken pains to point out. Of greater interest than stability of a given behavior across occasions is the degree of consistency among *different* actions assumed to reflect the same disposition. Stability of this kind has usually been termed "cross-situational consistency" since different actions, even if in the same behavioral domain, almost inevitably are performed in different contexts and at different points in time. Nevertheless, it is important to realize that returning books on time to the library, for example, differs from punctuality in handing in written assignments not only in terms of the context of the behavior but also, and perhaps more importantly, in terms of the particular activity involved (cf. Jackson and Paunonen, 1985).

According to the principle of aggregation, consistency across different kinds of behaviors and situations can also be obtained by means of aggregation. Evidence in support of this idea has long been available in the convergent validation of attitude scales and personality trait measures. As we saw in Chapter 1, properly constructed

attitude and personality scales consist of carefully selected items that assess specific (verbal) responses. Consistent with the principle of aggregation, however, these specific responses are aggregated over all items in the questionnaire to yield the attitude or trait scores. As expected, different multi-item measures of a given attitude or personality characteristic are routinely found to yield comparable results, with convergent validities typically in the 0.60–0.80 range. Edwards and Abbott (1973a, 1973b) and Lorr *et al.* (1977) reported data in general support of the convergent validity of various personality traits measured by different personality inventories. As a specific example, consider the study by Jaccard (1974). Scales taken from Jackson's (1967) Personality Research Form and from the California Psychological Inventory (Gough, 1957) were used to assess dominance in a sample of college students. The correlation between the two multi-item scales was found to be 0.75.

Comparing two different scaling techniques (Likert and Thurstone scaling), Edwards and Kenney (1946) provided evidence for the convergent validity of attitude measures. The original pool of items designed by Thurstone and Chave (1929) to assess attitudes toward the church was used to construct a Likert scale and two parallel forms of a Thurstone scale. The two forms of the Thurstone scale were found to correlate 0.72 and 0.92 with the Likert scale. Similarly, and again in the area of attitudes toward religion, Fishbein and Ajzen (1974) reported a high degree of convergent validity among four different types of standard multi-item scales: Thurstone, Likert, Guttman, and the semantic differential. Correlations among the four measures of attitude toward religion ranged from 0.64 to 0.79. This study also provided evidence for consistency among multiple-act indices of *behavior*, although the behaviors in question were self-reports rather than observations of overt actions. The college students who participated in the research were given a list of 100 behaviors dealing with matters of religion and were asked to check the behaviors they had performed. The list of behaviors included praying before or after meals, taking a religious course for credit, and dating a person against parents' wishes. By applying different scaling methods to the behavioral self-reports, three multiple-act indices of religious behavior were constructed. The correlations among these three aggregate measures of behavior ranged from 0.63 to 0.79.

The research reviewed thus far showed behavioral consistency at the aggregate level, but the responses that were aggregated were all obtained by means of questionnaires. Perhaps more convincing, therefore, would be data demonstrating consistency between aggregates based on nonverbal behaviors. Ironically, evidence of this kind was already reported by Hartshorne and May (1928; Hartshorne *et al.*, 1929, 1930) in their studies of deceit and character. In the reports of their findings, Hartshorne and May focused on the rather low correlations between individual measures, and their research has therefore often been interpreted as demonstrating little behavioral consistency. However, they also found that batteries of tests measuring different kinds of cheating in the classroom were found to correlate quite highly with each other [see Rushton *et al.* (1983) and Epstein and O'Brien (1985) for discussions of this research].

Strong evidence for consistency of behavioral aggregates was also reported in a more recent study by Small *et al.* (1983). These investigators joined four small groups of adolescents as counselors on a 30-day wilderness trip and recorded the youngsters' behaviors for 2 hours each day. The actions recorded fell into two broad categories: eight different kinds of dominance behaviors (e.g. verbal directive, physical assertiveness, verbal or physical threat) and five different kinds of pro-social behaviors (e.g. physical assistance, sharing, verbal support). Moreover, behavioral observations were obtained in three different contexts: setting up and dismantling the camp, activities surrounding meals (including preparation and clean-up), and free time. Multiple-act aggregates were computed for each type of behavior (dominance and pro-social) in each of the three settings, and the data were analyzed separately for each of the four groups. Cross-situational consistency of behavioral aggregates was found to be very high. For dominance behavior, correlations between different settings ranged from 0.33 to 0.95, with a mean of 0.73, and for pro-social behavior the range was 0.48 to 0.99, with a mean correlation of 0.79.

Finally, it has been shown that behavioral aggregates are relatively stable over time even when the individual behaviors of which the aggregates are comprised have little temporal stability (Sroufe and Waters, 1977; Waters, 1978). Interactions between mothers and their children were observed when the children were 12 months old and again when they were 18 months old. The behavioral category of primary interest were responses on the part of the children indicating attachment as opposed to avoidance. A total of 28 discrete actions were rated that had to do with smiling and looking at mother, vocalizing, following and clinging. The stabilities of individual behaviors over the 6-month period were largely nonsignificant, ranging from −0.16 to 0.46. In contrast, the correlations for behavioral aggregates were significant and quite high. Thus, maintaining contact showed a correlation of 0.72 over the 6-month period, avoiding proximity a correlation of 0.62, and resisting contact a correlation of 0.51. Sroufe (1979, p. 838) described the advantage of aggregation very clearly:

> Individual babies cried less or more, sought more or less contact, showed a toy to mother one time, brought a toy another time, but in some way the overall pattern of behavior indicative of a secure attachment relationship was revealed on both occasions.

### Predictive validity for behavioral aggregates

The aggregation principle also implies that general trait and attitude measures should permit prediction of equally general measures of behavior. That is, we should expect a strong association between multiple-act indices of behavior and standard measures of attitudes or personality traits. The former reflect the general disposition in the form of conative response tendencies while the latter use verbal questionnaire responses, typically falling into the cognitive and affective categories, to infer the same underlying disposition. Several investigations have provided support for the predictive validity of traits and attitudes in relation to behavioral aggregates. Consider, again, the Fishbein and Ajzen (1974) study. Each of the 100 self-reports of religious behavior (representing 100 single-act criteria), the three scaled aggregates, as well as the sum over the total set of behaviors (representing four multiple-act criteria), were correlated with each of the four standard, multi-item measures of attitude toward religion. As is typically found to be the case, prediction of single actions from global attitudes was largely unsuccessful. Although a few attitude–behavior correlations were as high as 0.40, most were rather low and not significant. The average correlation between attitudes toward religion and single behaviors was about 0.14. In marked contrast, the same global measures of attitude correlated highly and significantly with the aggregate indices of religious behavior; these correlations ranged from 0.53 to 0.73, and the mean correlation was 0.63.

Very similar results were reported in the area of activism concerning abortion (Werner, 1978). Werner assessed general attitudes toward abortion on demand among male and female respondents. In addition, the respondents were asked to report the extent to which they had performed each of 83 activities related to abortion. Among these activities were "trying to convince a friend or acquaintance that abortion should be greatly restricted or prohibited," "encouraging a woman with an unwanted pregnancy to have an abortion," and "circulating an anti-abortion petition." Consistent with the principle of aggregation, the attitude toward abortion was found to be a highly accurate predictor of a multiple-act index based on all 83 activities. For the total sample of respondents, the attitude–behavior correlation was 0.78.

Finally, Sjöberg (1982) obtained two measures of attitude toward aid to developing countries among male and female college students in Göteborg. These attitude measures were then used to predict a summary index of various self-reported behaviors, including "participation in Red Cross activities related to developing countries" and "corresponding with a person in a developing country." The correlations between the two measures of attitude and the multiple-act criterion in this study were found to be 0.49 and 0.43.

Following closely the procedures employed by Fishbein and Ajzen (1974), Jaccard (1974) examined the relation between the personality trait of dominance and self-reports of dominant behavior. As mentioned earlier, the female undergraduates who participated in Jaccard's study completed two personality scales designed to assess dominance. In addition, they were asked to indicate which of 40 behaviors in the domain of dominance they had performed. Among the behaviors listed were arguing with a teacher, initiating a discussion in class, and intentionally letting your boyfriend beat you at something. A multiple-act measure of dominance behavior was obtained by summing over the 40 actions. Prediction of single behaviors from the general personality trait measures was again rather poor. On average, the correlation between the two personality measures of dominance and the various dominant or submissive behaviors was about 0.20. Much greater success, however, was achieved in predicting the general tendency to behave in a dominant manner; the two personality measures correlated 0.58 and 0.64 with the multiple-act aggregate.

It can be argued as before that the weakness of these investigations is their reliance on self-reports of behavior (cf. Schuman and John-son, 1976). A study of Weigel and Newman (1976), however, showed the same pattern of results for observations of nonverbal behavior. These investigators used a multi-item scale designed to measure attitudes toward environmental quality and, 3–8 months later, observed 14 behaviors related to the environment. The be-haviors involved signing and circulating three different petitions concerning environmental issues, participating in a litter pick-up program, and participating in a recycling program on eight separate occasions. In addition to these 14 single-act, single-observation criteria, Weigel and Newman constructed four behavioral aggre-gates: one based on petition-signing behaviors, one on litter pick-ups, one on recycling, and one overall index based on all 14 observations. Prediction of each single observation from the general attitude measure was quite weak; the average correlation was 0.29 and not significant. The aggregates over occasions, based on multiple observations of single actions, showed a mean correlation of mod-erate magnitude with the general attitude ($r = 0.42$), while the multiple-act index over all 14 observations correlated 0.62 with the same attitude measure.

Strong associations between general measures of attitude and an aggregate index of behavior directed at the object of the attitude can also be found in a very different domain. Bandura *et al.* (1969) assessed attitudes toward snakes by means of two standard attitude scales. The avoidance behavior of undergraduates was then recorded with respect to a graded series of behaviors involving various interactions with a snake. These interactions ranged from approaching the snake in an enclosed glass cage to passively permit-ting the snake to crawl in one's lap. Following the behavior, attitudes were reassessed. Both attitude measures were found to predict the behavioral criterion with a high degree of accuracy. When adminis-tered prior to the behavior, the two attitude scales showed correla-tions of 0.73 and 0.56 with the multiple-act aggregate. Measured after the behavior, the corresponding correlations were 0.87 and 0.70.

Finally, as with respect to attitudes, there is also some evidence for an increase in the predictive validity of personality trait measures as a result of behavioral aggregation (McGowan and Gormly, 1976). Undergraduate fraternity members judged each fellow member as being or not being energetic or physically active. The proportion of positive ratings was taken as a measure of each participant's standing on this trait. Five behavioral self-reports (e.g. time spent on sports, longest distance ever walked, longest distance ever run) and five observations of actual behavior (e.g. speed of walking, rate of speed going upstairs, rate of head movements) were available. The correlations between the trait and the 10 individual behaviors ranged from 0.13 to 0.64, with an average of 0.42. After aggregation, the five self-reports of behavior had a correlation of 0.65 with the energism trait and the sum of the five observed behaviors correlated 0.70 with the trait. Finally, the correlation between the trait and an aggregate measure of behavior based on all 10 activities was 0.74.

## Aggregation and the question of consistency

Chapter 2 reviewed some empirical research that showed a lack of behavioral consistency and poor predictive validity of attitude and trait measures. Findings of this kind have been interpreted as evidence against the existence of stable behavioral dispositions, but the data reviewed in the present chapter concerning the effects of behavioral aggregation should lay this pessimistic conclusion to rest. Clearly, it is possible to obtain high behavioral (i.e. cross-situational) consistency, as well as impressive predictive validity, as long as the behavioral criteria used are broadly representative of the disposition under consideration.

The issues involved are closely related to questions of measurement reliability and validity. Factors that influence a given behavior, but that are of no particular interest to the investigator, are considered "error," and are said to contribute to unreliability or invalidity of measurement. To be sure, what is "error" in one investigation may be the focus of study in another. Variations in mood, ambient temperature, noise level, and other incidental factors are usually of little concern in attempts to predict behavior from attitudes or personality traits, but in other areas of research they constitute legitimate and important topics of investigation (e.g. Dulany, 1968; Eagly 1974; Isen and Levin, 1972). Nevertheless, the effects of mood, distracting factors like noise, etc., may be considered irrelevant and may be thought of as introducing unreliability if the investigator's interests lie elsewhere.

It is of course not inconceivable that we might be interested in understanding the unique set of circumstances that cause a given action in a specific context, on a given occasion. If so, we may well find that temporary moods, unanticipated distractions, situational demands, and so on, account for a large proportion of the behavioral variance. The typical finding of little or no consistency among individual behaviors observed on single occasions, and their low correlations with measures of general attitudes and personality traits, attest to the relative unimportance of stable dispositions in comparison to the effects of incidental factors that are unique to a given occasion. However, with such notable exceptions as voting in an election, we are rarely interested in explaining performance or nonperformance of a single action on a given occasion. Instead, we are usually concerned with relatively stable tendencies to perform (or not to perform) a given behavior: drinking alcohol, rather than drinking a glass of champagne at a New Year's party in the company of friends; using birth control pills, rather than taking the pill on a given day; and so on. Incidental factors uniquely associated with any given occasion are therefore mostly of little concern. Aggregation across a sufficient number of occasions serves the purpose of reducing to an acceptable minimum error variance produced by factors of this kind.

By the same token, variance associated with different actions that are assumed to reflect the same underlying disposition may also be considered a source of error. This is legitimate whenever we are interested in a broad behavioral trend, rather than in understanding the factors that result in a tendency to perform (or not to perform) a given action. Thus, we may want to study aggression rather than administration of electric shocks in a learning situation, or discrimination rather than conformity with a minority group member's judgments. This requires use of multiple-act aggregates that reflect the broad behavioral trend in question. As expected, such broad response dispositions are found to be relatively stable across time and context, and they tend to correlate well with equally broad questionnaire measures of attitudes and personality traits.

The aggregation solution to the consistency problem was anticipated as early as 1931 by Thurstone, who pointed out that two persons may hold the same attitude toward some object but that "their overt actions (may) take quite different forms which have one thing in common, namely, that they are about equally favorable toward the object" (p. 262). It would have come as no surprise to Thurstone that general attitudes are largely unrelated to specific actions, but that they are closely related to multiple-act indices of behavioral trends. As is true of verbal measures of attitudes and personality traits, aggregate measures of behavior provide *quantitative* indicators of the underlying response disposition. Although the intensity of a general attitude or personality trait cannot predict whether or not a particular behavior will be performed, it can predict the strength of the behavioral tendency, as reflected in the aggregate response measure.

Note that not all behaviors can be aggregated with equal effectiveness into a multiple-act measure (see Epstein, 1983b; Jackson and Paunonen, 1985). It is not sufficient that the behaviors to be combined into an index appear to reflect the same underlying disposition, i.e. that they have face validity. Like items on a personality or attitude scale, they must be shown, by means of acceptable psychometric procedures, to share common variance and thus to be indicative of the same underlying disposition. The importance of selecting appropriate behaviors for aggregation is demonstrated in a series of studies by Buss and Craik (1980, 1981, 1984). In one of their investigations, for example, respondents in a pilot study rated each of 100 behaviors in terms of how good an example of dominance they thought it was (Buss and Craik, 1980). The average rating served as a measure of the act's prototypicality in relation to the trait of dominance. On the basis of these scores, the behaviors were divided into four categories of 25 behaviors each, from the most to the least prototypically dominant acts. In the main study, respondents completed two personality scales assessing dominance and also provided a self-rating of dominance on a 7-point scale. In addition, they reported the frequency with which they had, in the past, performed each of the 100 dominance behaviors. Four multiple-act indices were constructed by summing over the self-reports in the four prototypicality categories. As is usually the case, correlations between the three standard measures of dominance and each of the 100 single behaviors were very low, averaging between 0.10 and 0.20, depending on the measure used to assess the dominance trait. The correlations with the multiple-act aggregate based on the least prototypically dominant acts, however, were not much better – they ranged from 0.05 to 0.33. Only when the behaviors aggregated were considered very good examples of the dominance trait, i.e. when they appeared clearly relevant to the disposition, did the correlations between assessed dominance and behavioral trends in the dominance domain attain appreciable magnitude, ranging from 0.25 to 0.67.

In short, evidence for consistency and, hence, for the existence of relatively stable response dispositions, is obtained when behaviors are appropriately selected and aggregated into multiple-act measures of behavioral tendencies. Mischel and Peake (1982a), however, reject this approach on the grounds that

> cross-situational aggregation also often has the undesirable effect of canceling out some of the most valuable data about a person. It misses the point completely for the psychologist interested in the unique patterning of the individual by treating within-person variance, and indeed the context itself, as if it were "error" (p. 738).

Although not inconsistent with the view of aggregation described above, this criticism fails to appreciate the fact that, according to the principle of aggregation, broad response dispositions (traits, attitudes) are largely irrelevant to an understanding of specific actions performed in a given context. Lack of consistency between global dispositional measures and specific actions, or between different specific acts, does not constitute evidence that the concept of personality traits as broad response dispositions is untenable (Mischel, 1968) or that there are no stable attitudes within an individual that influence verbal expressions as well as actions (Wicker, 1969). Rather, in view of the aggregation principle, such inconsistency reflects poor operationalization of "behavior." To have expected strong relations between global measures of personality or attitude and any particular action may have been rather naive. In fact, such an expectation contradicts our definitions of attitude and personality trait as general behavioral dispositions.

It should be clear at the same time, however, that aggregation has its limitations. Through aggregation across actions and contexts we can demonstrate cross-situational consistency of behavior, as well as consistency between verbal and nonverbal indicators of an underlying disposition. But, obviously, aggregation does not open the way for an understanding of the factors that influence performance or nonperformance of a particular action. Returning to the hit-and-run accident described at the beginning of this chapter, if we are interested in the determinants of the driver's failure to come to the assistance of the victim, it will serve no useful purpose to treat this behavior as an instance of irresponsibility and to compute a broad index of various actions in the responsibility domain. Such a multiple-act index should, in fact, be stable across situations and correlate well with a questionnaire measure of responsibility, but it adds little to our understanding of the factors involved in hit-and-run incidents. Clearly, we will need to approach this issue in a different manner if we are to deal with the determinants of individual behaviors.

## Summary and conclusions

In contrast to the pessimistic conclusions reached by many personality and social psychologists in the 1960s and reviewed in Chapter 2, the present chapter showed that it is possible to demonstrate consistency of behavior across occasions and situations and to obtain an accurate prediction of behavior from verbal attitude and personality trait measures. Behavioral consistency and predictive validity were shown to be the usual outcome of aggregating a variety of specific behavioral tendencies. The resulting multiple-act criterion is relatively free of the influence of factors incidental to any given situation or action and it is thus a reasonably "pure" reflection of the general attitudinal or personality disposition of interest to the investigator. It is for this reason that multiple-act criteria are stable across situations and correlate well with equally general verbal measures of the disposition.

Although re-establishing some degree of confidence in the trait and attitude concepts, the principle of aggregation limits our ability to predict and understand human action to the domain of multiple-act criteria. The next three chapters of this book deal in different ways with the problem of using dispositional variables to predict and explain specific behavioral tendencies.

## Suggestions for further readings

1. Fishbein, M. and Ajzen, I. (1974). Attitudes toward objects as predictors of single and multiple behavioral criteria. *Psychological Review*, **81**, 59–74. This article discusses the principle of aggregation and presents empirical support for the principle in the context of the attitude–behavior relation.
2. Mischel, W. and Peake, P. K. (1982). Beyond *déjà vu* in the search for cross-situational consistency. *Psychological Review*, **89**, 730–55. This article provides a critical response to the use of aggregation in personality research.
3. Small, S. A., Zeldin, R. S. and Savin-Williams, R. C. (1983). In search of

personality traits: A multimethod analysis of naturally occurring pro-social and dominance behavior. *Journal of Personality*, **5 1**, 1–16. A nice illustration of the utility of the aggregation principle in personality research.

# 4 / MODERATING VARIABLES

There's no limit to how complicated things can get on account of one thing always leading to another.

*E. B. White*

Our discussions in the preceding chapters have culminated in two general conclusions. First, application of the aggregation principle has demonstrated that it is appropriate to postulate broad attitudinal and personality dispositions, dispositions that are stable over time and that permit reasonably accurate prediction of multiple-act behavioral indices. Secondly, however, it has also become quite clear that broad attitude and personality trait measures correlate very poorly with individual behaviors or behavioral tendencies. Individual behaviors, even if observed repeatedly, are typically performed in a particular context or situation appropriate for the behavior in question. Thus, cheating on exams occurs mainly in classroom situations, whereas shoplifting is, by definition, tied to commercial retail establishments. In other words, different behaviors, even if they belong to a common domain such as honesty–dishonesty, are performed in different situations. Situational variability is even greater, of course, if we consider single unaggregated instances of behavior. In addition to the individual's general predisposition, therefore, various features of the situation can affect the performance or nonperformance of a given behavior. By aggregating over actions and situations we eliminate these complications, but they re-emerge when we are dealing with a single behavior or with a behavioral tendency over time.

Not only can situational variables have an impact on a specific behavior independent of whatever stable dispositions people bring to the situation, they can also *moderate* the effects of attitudes or personality traits. That is, people's characteristic traits or attitudes may influence their behavior in some situations but not in others.

Consider, for example, the case of a person who is taken ill while walking in the street. A dispositional approach to human behavior might suggest that passers-by will offer help to the extent that they are altruistic. However, the effect of altruism on helping may depend on a variety of situational factors: whether the need for help is readily apparent, the sex and age of the person who was taken ill, the presence or absence of other people who could help, and so on. Situational characteristics of this kind may serve to "activate" implicit dispositional tendencies (Schwartz, 1977; Staub, 1974), and it is perhaps only when such activation occurs that people behave in accordance with their dispositions.

### Effects of moderating variables

It is possible to generalize the notion of moderating variables to other types of factors, in addition to the situation, that may also have an effect on the relation between general attitudes or personality traits and specific behaviors. According to the moderating variables approach, the extent to which a general disposition is reflected in overt action is subject to various contingencies. Attitudes and personality traits are thus assumed to interact with other variables in their effects on specific behaviors. This *interactionist* or *contingent consistency* position has been adopted both in the domain of personality (e.g. Bowers, 1973; Ekehammer, 1974; Endler and Magnusson, 1976) and in the domain of social psychology (e.g. Fazio and Zanna, 1981; Snyder, 1982; Warner and DeFleur, 1969; see also Sherman and Fazio, 1983, for a discussion of moderating variables in personality and social psychology). The factors that are said to interact with attitudes or personality traits may be grouped into four broad categories: characteristics of the individual, secondary characteristics of the disposition, circumstances surrounding performance of the behavior, and the nature of the behavior selected to represent the underlying disposition.

### *Individual differences as moderators*

The search for individual difference variables as moderators of the relation between dispositions and behavior is based on the assumption that consistency can be expected for some individuals but not for others. The efforts of many investigators have thus centered on identifying the characteristics of individuals that are likely to promote or undermine consistency. These efforts have produced a rather lengthy list of potential moderators, but as we shall see, empirical attempts to verify their operation have produced largely inconclusive results.

*Behavior-specific individual differences*

Arguing that not all trait dimensions are equally relevant to all people, Bem and Allen (1974, p. 512) hypothesized that "Individuals who identify themselves as consistent on a particular trait dimension will in fact be more consistent cross-situationally than those who identify themselves as highly variable." People who are found to behave consistently in one behavioral domain may be inconsistent in another. Thus we can expect to predict behavior only for "some of the people some of the time." To test these ideas, Bem and Allen examined the behavior of college students in the domains of friendliness and conscientiousness. Participants rated the extent to which they thought they *varied* from one situation to another in how friendly and outgoing they were and in how conscientious they were. They were then divided, at the median, into consistent and inconsistent subgroups, separately for each behavioral domain. The participants' standing on the two trait dimensions (friendliness and conscientiousness) was assessed by means of a simple 7-point scale and by means of a multi-item self-report behavioral inventory. With respect to each trait dimension, ratings were provided by the participants themselves, by their parents, and by their peers. In addition, several nonverbal measures of behavior were obtained: friendliness displayed in the course of a group discussion and spontaneously while sitting with a confederate in a waiting room; and conscientiousness expressed in the prompt return of course evaluations, completion of course readings, and neatness of personal appearance and of living quarters. Finally, participants also completed an inventory assessing introversion–extraversion, as a possible dispositional predictor of friendliness.

Differences in consistency were explored by comparing the correlations of the high and low variability subgroups.[1] Results in the domain of friendliness supported Bem and Allen's hypothesis. One of the supportive findings had to do with inter-rater reliability of friendliness, i.e. with the correlations among ratings of friendliness provided by the participants themselves, by their parents, and by their peers. These correlations were significantly higher for individuals who considered themselves consistently friendly than for individuals who reported that their friendliness varied from situation to situation. Also, there was evidence that the introversion–extraversion scale was a somewhat better predictor of a person's rated friendliness and of nonverbal behavior in this domain for low variability ($r = 0.25-0.77$) than for high variability individuals ($r = -0.12-0.65$). Finally, the correlation between friendliness in a group discussion and spontaneous friendliness was stronger in the low ($r = 0.73$) than in the high ($r = 0.30$) variability group.

The results with respect to conscientiousness, however, did not provide as clear a picture. An analysis identical to that performed with respect to friendliness revealed no differences between low and high consistency subgroups. Consequently, Bem and Allen decided to divide participants into consistent versus inconsistent subgroups on the basis of variability in responses to the multi-item self-report behavioral inventory. When this was done, the expected differences in inter-rater reliabilities again emerged, but the correlations among the three objective measures of behavior still failed to show the expected pattern. The range of correlations here was from $-0.01$ to $-0.11$ for respondents low in variability and from $0.18$ to $-0.61$ for highly variable respondents.

In a replication of the Bem and Allen (1974) study, Mischel and Peake (1982a) presented data on the correlations among their 19 behaviors in the conscientiousness domain described in Chapter 2; the correlations were computed separately for individuals who had judged themselves low as opposed to high in variability. The expected differences between the subgroups failed to materialize. The mean correlation was $0.15$ in the low variability group and $0.10$ in the high variability group. Finally, a thorough attempt by Chaplin and Goldberg (1984) to replicate the Bem and Allen (1974) findings also resulted in failure. These investigators considered eight personality traits: friendliness, conscientiousness, honesty, sensitivity, assertiveness, activity level, emotional stability, and cultural sophistication. Furthermore, they used three methods to divide respondents into low and high consistency subgroups: Bem and Allen's two methods, as well as a division on the basis of self-rated consistency with respect to various specific behaviors in each of the trait domains. And, like Bem and Allen, they compared the subgroups in terms of inter-rater reliability and in terms of correlations among nonverbal measures of specific actions in each domain. The results revealed few significant differences between high and low consistency subgroups, irrespective of the method used to partition the sample, and there was no systematic pattern to the differences that did emerge.

*Personality traits*

In contrast to the approach advocated by Bem and Allen, which looks for individual differences in consistency that are tied to a given behavioral domain, some researchers have attempted to identify stable personality characteristics that lead certain individuals to exhibit strong consistency between verbal and nonverbal indicators of a disposition, and others to exhibit little consistency of this kind, irrespective of the behavioral domain under consideration. A case in point is the tendency toward *self-monitoring* (Snyder, 1974, 1979). People high on this dimension are said to be rather pragmatic, acting in accordance with the requirements of the situation. In contrast, low self-monitoring individuals are assumed to act on the basis of principles, in accordance with their personal values, preferences, and convictions. It follows that we should find stronger attitude–behavior and trait–behavior relations among the latter than among the former.

Although it did not include a measure of overt behavior, Snyder and Swann's (1976) study of mock jury judgments is often taken as support for the idea that self-monitoring moderates the relation between attitudes and actions. The self-monitoring tendencies of college students were assessed by means of Snyder's (1974) personality scale, and the sample was divided at the median score into subgroups high and low on this trait dimension. A standard scale measuring attitudes toward affirmative action was administered and, 2 weeks later, participants were asked to reach a verdict in a mock court case involving alleged sex discrimination. The case was brought by a woman who had been rejected for a university faculty position in favor of a male applicant. The materials presented to the respondents included summaries of the applicants' biographies and of the arguments advanced in court on behalf of the plaintiff and the university. For the total sample of participants, the correlation between attitudes toward affirmative action and the mock jurors' verdicts was a modest 0.22. However, as expected, it was stronger for individuals low in self-monitoring ($r = 0.42$) than for high self-monitoring individuals ($r = 0.03$).

The parallel expectation that people's self-monitoring tendency influences the predictive validity of personality trait measures has also received some empirical support. Becherer and Richard (1978) asked college students to express their preferences for private brands of eight different products (i.e. brands offered by retailers) as compared to national brands of the same products. The products used were cologne or perfume, mouthwash, complexion aids, alcoholic beverages, vitamins, pocket calculators, coffee, and candy bars. Average preference ratings were correlated with 18 personality traits assessed by means of the California Personality Inventory. Six of the 18 traits were found to make significant contributions to the prediction of preference ratings: tolerance, responsibility, socialization, achievement, dominance, and intellectual efficiency. Snyder's scale was again used to divide participants into low and high self-monitoring subgroups. Multiple correlations between personality traits and preference ratings ranged from 0.65 to 0.80 for participants with low scores on the self-monitoring scale and from 0.33 to 0.42 for participants with high self-monitoring scores.

However, other studies, looking at behavior rather than judgments or preferences, have not always been able to demonstrate the moderating effects of self-monitoring tendencies. For example, Zuckerman and Reis (1978) used attitudes toward donating blood at a forthcoming blood donation campaign to predict actual blood donations. For the total sample of respondents, the attitude–behavior correlation was found to be 0.36, and there was no significant difference between individuals high and low in self-monitoring tendency. Likewise, little evidence for the moderating effects of self-monitoring was reported by Ajzen *et al.* (1982) who attempted to predict whether or not college students would vote in a forthcoming presidential election on the basis of several dispositional measures: social responsibility, liberalism–conservatism, political involvement, attitudes toward voting in the election, and intentions to vote. They also tried to predict marijuana use among the same students from social responsibility, attitudes toward smoking marijuana, and intentions to smoke marijuana. Only the intention–behavior correlations were significantly affected by self-monitoring, with low self-monitoring individuals displaying stronger correlations than high self-monitoring individuals. Self-monitoring failed to have a consistent moderating effect on any of the attitude–behavior or trait–behavior correlations.

Finally, Snyder and Kendzierski (1982) assessed students' general attitudes toward psychological research in an attempt to predict their volunteering to participate in such research. The students overheard two confederates express the opinion that volunteering was either a matter of personal choice or that it depended on one's attitude toward psychological research. In neither condition did the self-monitoring tendency significantly affect the magnitude of the correlations between attitudes and behavior; these correlations were 0.50 and 0.70 for low and high self-monitoring individuals, respectively, in the attitude-relevant condition, and 0.20 and 0.30 in the personal choice condition.

A second general characteristic that is said to moderate the degree of consistency between dispositions and behavior is *private self-consciousness*. This trait refers to people's awareness of private aspects of themselves including, importantly, their feelings, motives, and values (cf. Buss, 1980). Due to their greater awareness of these internal states, people high in private self-consciousness are assumed to behave more in accordance with their dispositions than do people low on this dimension.

Empirical support for this hypothesis can be found in a study that dealt with the relation between dispositions toward aggressiveness or hostility and aggressive behavior in the laboratory (Scheier *et al.*, 1978). Dispositions were assessed by means of a multi-item aggressiveness/hostility inventory and Buss's (1961) aggression paradigm was used to observe aggressive behavior. In this paradigm, participants are led to believe that the study investigates the use of punishment, in the form of electric shocks, to improve performance on a learning task. The naive participant is to serve as teacher and another student (actually an assistant to the investigator) serves as pupil. Each time the pupil makes a mistake, the teacher is to administer a shock of an intensity selected by the teacher. In reality, of course, no shocks are administered. The pupil goes through a series of learning trials and makes a predetermined number of errors. The average intensity of the shocks ostensibly administered is taken as a measure of the aggressiveness of the participant's behavior. In the present study, there were 25 "error" trials. Private self-consciousness was assessed by means of a personality scale developed by Fenigstein *et al.* (1975), and participants were selected from the top and bottom thirds of the distribution. Consistent with expectations, the correlation between the questionnaire measure of aggressiveness and behavior in the aggression paradigm was 0.34 for the total sample, 0.09 for participants low in private self-consciousness, and 0.66 for participants high in private self-consciousness.

Underwood and Moore (1981) replicated these findings with respect to a different behavioral domain but also obtained some unexpected results. Same-sex pairs of college students talked freely to form an impression of the other person. At the conclusion, each person rated his or her partner on overall sociability and on seven items concerning the extent to which the partner had displayed specific behaviors reflective of sociability. The two sets of ratings were combined to obtain a general measure of sociability during interaction. In addition, each participant provided the same ratings for his or her own behavior. Two behavioral sociability scores were thus available, one based on peer ratings, the other on self ratings. The dispositional predictor was a personality measure of sociability obtained prior to the interaction, and private self-consciousness was assessed by means of the Fenigstein *et al.* (1975) scale. The correlation between the questionnaire measure of sociability and peer ratings of sociable behavior was, as expected, stronger in the case of participants high in private self-consciousness ($r = 0.44$) than for participants low on this dimension ($r = 0.03$). However, when self-ratings of sociability during interaction served as the behavioral dependent variable, the pattern was reversed: $r = 0.27$ and $0.61$, respectively. No convincing explanation for this reversal is readily available.

The final individual difference variable to be discussed as a possible moderator of the relation between general dispositions and specific action tendencies is a person's *need for cognition*. According to the elaboration likelihood model of attitude change (Petty and Cacioppo, 1981, 1986), individuals who form their attitudes after carefully scrutinizing available evidence exhibit stronger attitude–behavior correlations than individuals who do little "central processing" of this kind but instead base their attitudes on relatively superficial external cues. Furthermore, Cacioppo *et al.* (1986a) reasoned that people high in need for cognition, i.e. people who have a strong need to understand and make reasonable the world they experience (Cohen *et al.*, 1955), are more likely to process information carefully than are people with low standing on this dimension. Taken together, these ideas imply a stronger attitude–behavior correlation among people high as compared to low in need for cognition.

In a study designed to test this hypothesis, Cacioppo *et al.* (1986a,

Experiment 2) assessed the need for cognition by means of a personality scale and examined correlations between attitudinal preferences for candidates in a presidential election and actual voting choice. Consistent with expectations this correlation was found to be 0.86 for people high in need for cognition, but only 0.41 for people low in need for cognition.

In conclusion, the search for individual differences as moderating variables has produced rather mixed results. Attempts to identify individual differences in behavioral variability that could account for consistent or inconsistent behavior in a given domain have been largely unsuccessful. The moderating effect of self-monitoring is found to be quite tenuous; a low self-monitoring tendency is sometimes accompanied by greater predictive validity, but at other times there are no differences between high and low self-monitoring individuals. Empirical findings are somewhat more encouraging with respect to private self-consciousness. When private self-consciousness is high, behavior is more likely to be guided by general attitudes or personality traits than when self-consciousness is low. This effect seems to depend, however, on whether the measure of behavior is based on self-reports or on reports provided by observers. Finally, the need for cognition has been shown to moderate the attitude–behavior relation, but more research is needed to establish the generality of this finding.

## Secondary characteristics of the disposition

The second class of moderating variables to be considered are secondary characteristics of a disposition. Variables of this kind have been examined primarily with respect to attitudes. In addition to assessing the strength and direction of an attitude, it is also possible to measure its internal structure, a person's involvement in the attitude domain, the confidence with which the attitude is held, the way it was formed, and so on (see Raden, 1985, for a review). Each of these factors may influence the magnitude of the relation between general attitudes and specific behavioral tendencies.

### Internal structure
The multidimensional view of attitude described in Chapter 1 holds that attitudes are composed of cognitive, affective, and conative response tendencies. As noted in Chapter 2, the question of interest is

the degree to which the different components of attitude are evaluatively consistent with each other. Specifically, Rosenberg (1965) postulated that affective–cognitive consistency is a prerequisite for effective action. To test this idea, R. Norman (1975) examined the moderating effects of consistency between an attitude's affective and cognitive components in a series of three experiments. It was expected that attitude–behavior correlations would be stronger when the two components were consistent rather than inconsistent with each other. The affective component of undergraduates' attitudes toward acting as subjects in psychological research was measured by means of a 9-point favorability scale and, in the third study, also by means of a 16-item evaluative semantic differential. The cognitive component was indexed by an expectancy-value scale (see p. 32) based on 12 beliefs regarding the consequences of participating in psychological research. The two measures were each rank-ordered and, following Rosenberg's (1968) suggestion, the absolute difference between the ranks was taken as an index of affective–cognitive inconsistency. A median split partitioned participants into low and high internal consistency subgroups. To obtain measures of behavior, participants in the first two studies were invited to sign up for an experiment (signing up as well as actual attendance were scored), and in the third study they were recruited for two additional sessions while already participating in an experiment. The results provided partial support for the hypothesis. Across the three studies, the average correlation between behavior and the *affective* measure of attitude was 0.54 under conditions of high affective–cognitive consistency, and significantly lower (mean $r = -0.08$) when affect and cognition were relatively inconsistent with each other. With respect to the correlations between behavior and the *cognitive* measure of attitude, however, a significant difference between the high and low affective–cognitive consistency subgroups was obtained only in the third study (mean $r = 0.47$ and 0.28, respectively).

Moreover, Fazio and Zanna (1978a) failed to find any moderating effect of affective–cognitive consistency in a replication of Norman's experiments with only minor modifications. To obtain an overall measure of attitude, Fazio and Zanna combined the measures of the affective and cognitive components into a single score. Their analysis resulted in a significant correlation ($r = 0.32$) between the overall attitude and volunteering to serve as a subject in psychological research, but this correlation was not influenced by the degree of affective–cognitive consistency.

A different approach to the question of an attitude's internal consistency was adopted by Schlegel and DiTecco (1982). On the basis of a 20-item attitude scale toward marijuana administered to high school students, nonusers or initial users were shown to have less differentiated (i.e. more internally consistent) attitudes toward marijuana than occasional or regular users. Attitudes toward smoking marijuana, assessed by means of an evaluative semantic differential, were employed to predict self-reports of actual marijuana use. These attitude–behavior correlations were found to be stronger among relatively undifferentiated participants (the average attitude–behavior correlation across different subpopulations was 0.36) than among participants whose attitude structure was relatively complex (mean correlation 0.18).

*Information and reflection*
Another secondary characteristic of verbal attitude that is said to affect its relation to overt behavior is the amount of information on which the attitude is based. Davidson *et al.* (1985) conducted three studies that compared intention–behavior correlations among participants with varying amounts of information relevant to the behavior. The first two studies dealt with behavior in the political domain: voting choice among different candidates in a mayoral election and voting for or against certain legislative initiatives in a referendum. In the third study, behavioral intentions and actions of elderly citizens were assessed with respect to obtaining an influenza vaccination. In each case, intention–behavior consistency was found to be significantly greater for respondents who were more informed about the issues involved, or who reported being more informed.

Somewhat related to the question of the amount of information available to individuals is the extent to which attitudes are expressed after sufficient reflection. It is usually assumed that people are more likely to act in accordance with their attitudes if they "think before they act" (Snyder, 1982). Snyder and Swann's (1976) research on mock juror judgments in a sex discrimination court case mentioned earlier provided support for this idea. Prior to delivering their verdicts, one-half of the participants were encouraged to reflect upon their attitudes toward affirmative action. In this condition, the correlation between general attitudes toward affirmative action and the specific verdict was 0.58, as opposed to a correlation of 0.07 in a control group without prior reflection.

This finding concerning the moderating effect of reflection is quite consistent with the research on such individual difference variables as self-consciousness, in that reflection on one's attitudes presumably brings about self-focused attention. However, a series of studies by Wilson *et al.* (1984) arrived at contradictory conclusions. The first of three studies employed an intellectual puzzles task, the second dealt with vacation snapshots, and the third with the relationships of dating couples. One-half of the participants in each study was asked to list reasons for their attitudes toward the behavioral target: why they found the different puzzles interesting or boring, why they enjoyed or did not enjoy watching the snapshots, and why their dating relationship was good or bad. The behavioral criteria in the three studies were the amount of time spent working on each puzzle type, nonverbal expressions of enjoyment while watching the snapshots, and status of the dating relationship about 9 months later. In each case, the attitude–behavior correlation was stronger (ranging from 0.53 to 0.57 across studies) when respondents were *not* asked to list reasons for their attitudes than when they were asked to do so (range of correlations: −0.05 to 0.17).

Realizing that their findings were inconsistent with previous research, Wilson *et al.* (1984) argued that whereas self-focused attention involves merely *observing* one's thoughts and feelings, i.e. focusing on them, participants in their studies were asked to *analyze* those thoughts and feelings, i.e. to find reasons for their attitudes. The investigators speculated that this difference may have been sufficient to produce the contradictory findings. In a follow-up study, Wilson and Dunn (1986) again demonstrated reduced attitude–behavior correlations when participants were asked to analyze their attitudes, but they failed to corroborate the finding that focusing on one's attitudes serves to improve behavioral prediction.

## Involvement

It stands to reason that people with a strong vested interest in a behavior are more likely to act on their attitudes than are people with little vested interest in the behavior. Sivacek and Crano (1982) tested this hypothesis in two experiments. The topic of investigation in the first study was a referendum to raise the State's legal drinking age to 21. College students were asked to indicate their positions with respect to this issue on a 7-point scale. As might be expected, most (72 of the 93 participants) were opposed to the proposal. A short time later they were contacted by phone and asked to volunteer to call voters and urge them to vote against the proposal. The age of the respondent was used to operationalize vested interest since younger students would be directly affected by the law, whereas older students would not, or would be affected for only a short time. The participants were therefore divided into three groups on the basis of their age. As predicted, the volunteering rate among respondents opposed to the proposal increased from 13% for students with a low vested interest to 47% for students with a high vested interest. For the total sample, the correlation between attitude toward the proposed change in law and the number of calls volunteered was 0.23. When computed separately for the three vested interest groups, the correlation rose from 0.16 in the lowest vested interest group to 0.19 in the moderate vested interest group and to 0.30 in the highest vested interest group. That the correlation was relatively weak even in the latter group can perhaps be attributed to the poor (single-item) attitude measure. It should also be noted, of course, that this attitude is quite general, whereas the behavior predicted was a specific action (volunteering to make telephone calls). A multiple-act measure of behavior with respect to the proposed law might have produced better results.

The second study reported by Sivacek and Crano (1982) provides some support for this idea. Undergraduate college students completed a scale designed to assess their attitudes toward instituting a comprehensive exam at their university as a prerequisite for graduation. Vested interest in the topic was measured by two questions concerning the likelihood that the respondent would have to take the exam (if instituted) and the extent to which instituting the exam would directly affect the respondent. On the basis of the sum of these two responses the participants were divided into three vested interest groups. The behavior observed was whether or not participants signed a petition opposing the proposed exam, whether or not they volunteered to help distribute petitions, write letters to newspapers, etc., and the number of hours of help they pledged. In addition, an aggregate measure of behavior was obtained by constructing a scale on the basis of these three actions. For the total sample of respondents, attitude–behavior correlations ranged from 0.34 to 0.43 for the three individual actions, while a correlation of 0.60 was obtained in the prediction of the behavioral aggregate. This again demonstrates the importance of aggregation to achieve strong attitude–behavior correlations. As to the effect of vested interest, the correlations between attitudes and individual actions ranged from 0.24 to 0.42 in the low vested interest group and from 0.60 to 0.74 in the high vested interest group. Using the behavioral aggregate score, this comparison showed correlations of 0.53 and 0.82, respectively.

A study by Regan and Fazio (1977), conducted during a housing shortage at Cornell University, can also be interpreted as demonstrating the moderating effect of vested interest or involvement. As a result of the housing problem, many freshmen were severely inconvenienced by being forced to spend their first few weeks of the fall semester in temporary, uncomfortable accommodation. Attitudes of freshmen toward the housing crisis were assessed by means of five attitudinal items and were found to be quite negative, irrespective of whether the student had been assigned to temporary or to permanent housing. Nevertheless, those assigned to temporary housing had a greater vested interest in remedial action. Six behavioral opportunities were provided to all students in the sample, among them signing a petition addressed to the administration, listing recommendations or suggestions for solving the crisis, and writing a letter to the Housing Office. The correlation between attitudes and an index based on all six behaviors was 0.42 in the high vested interest group and 0.04 in the low vested interest group.

Fazio and Zanna (1978a) used "latitude of rejection" to operationalize involvement in the topic of psychological research. The number of positions college students judged as objectionable on a 7-point *boring–interesting* scale was taken as an index of the latitude of rejection. The greater this latitude, the more involved a person is assumed to be (cf. Sherif and Hovland, 1961). A combination of the affective and cognitive instruments developed by R. Norman (1975) and described earlier was used to measure attitudes toward serving as a subject in psychological research. Toward the end of the experimental session participants were asked to join a subject pool from which volunteers would be drawn for psychological research. The behavioral criterion was the number of experiments in which a person volunteered to participate. Statistical analyses of the data showed a significant effect of attitude on behavior ($r = 0.32$) as well as a significant interaction between attitude and involvement. When the sample was divided into three groups of high, medium and low involvement, the attitude–behavior correlations in the respective subsamples were 0.52, 0.26 and 0.19.

## Confidence

Another secondary characteristic of an attitude is a person's degree of confidence in an expressed position. Several studies have obtained support for the moderating role of confidence. Perhaps the first empirical demonstration was provided by Warland and Sample (1973; Sample and Warland, 1973). The attitudes of college students toward student government were assessed by means of a 15-item Likert scale developed by Tittle and Hill (1967). After responding to all 15 items the participants were asked to read each item again and to rate, on a 5-point scale, how certain they were with respect to the response they had given to the item. Based on the sum of these certainty ratings, participants were divided into low- and high-confidence subgroups. Attitudes toward student government were used to predict participation in undergraduate student elections, ascertained from the voting list. The correlation between attitudes and voting was 0.26 for the total sample, 0.10 for respondents with low confidence in their attitudes, and 0.47 for respondents with high confidence.

A significant moderating effect of attitudinal confidence was also reported in the study by Fazio and Zanna (1978a), described above. In addition to expressing their positions, the participants rated, on a 9-point scale, how certain they felt about their attitudes toward volunteering to act as subjects. When the sample was split into three equal subgroups on the basis of these confidence ratings, the attitude–behavior correlation was found to be 0.08 for respondents with low confidence, and about 0.40 for respondents with moderate or high confidence.

Fazio and Zanna (1978b) also demonstrated the moderating effect of confidence by means of an experimental manipulation. As a measure of attitude, college students rated the interest value of each of five types of puzzles. They were then provided with bogus physiological feedback about the confidence with which they held their attitudes toward the different puzzles. One-half of the participants were told that they held their attitudes with a high degree of confidence, the other half that they held their attitudes with little confidence. Three measures of behavior were obtained during a 15-minute free-play situation: the order in which each puzzle type was attempted, the number of puzzles of each type attempted (out of the total available), and the amount of time spent on each type of puzzle. Within-subject correlations (across puzzle-types) were computed between attitudes and each measure of behavior. The average correlation (across the three behaviors and across participants) in the high confidence condition ($r = 0.60$) was significantly greater than the average correlation ($r = 0.44$) in the low confidence condition.

*Direct experience*
It has been suggested that the prediction of behavior from attitudes improves to the extent that the attitude is based on direct experience (Fazio and Zanna, 1978a, 1978b; Regan and Fazio, 1977; see also Fazio and Zanna, 1981, for a summary). Fazio and his associates have demonstrated the moderating effect of direct experience in two settings. In the first (Regan and Fazio, 1977), the relation between attitudes and behavior was examined with respect to the five types of intellectual puzzles mentioned above. In the indirect experience condition of the experiment, participants were given a description of each puzzle type and were shown previously solved examples of the puzzles. By way of contrast, in the direct experience condition, participants were given an opportunity actually to work on the same puzzles. As described earlier, expressed interest in each puzzle type served as a measure of attitude, and behavior (order and proportion of each puzzle type attempted) was assessed during a 15-minute free-play period. Correlations between attitudes and the two measures of behavior were 0.51 and 0.54 in the direct experience condition and 0.22 and 0.20 in the indirect experience condition.

A second study demonstrating the moderating effect of direct experience was reported by Fazio and Zanna (1978a). As we saw earlier, this study examined the relation between attitudes toward participating in psychological research and actual participation (by becoming a member of the subject pool and signing up for a certain number of experiments). The amount of direct experience in this situation was defined by the number of experiments in which a person had participated as a subject in the past. The attitude–behavior correlation was 0.42 in the top third of the prior experience subsample, 0.36 in the subsample with moderate prior experience, and −0.03 for the least experienced participants.

In conclusion, various lines of research have shown that an attitude's secondary characteristics moderate the relation between general attitudes and specific behaviors. Information and reflection, involvement, and confidence have all been found to increase the attitude's predictive validity. The results of experiments on the moderating effects of direct experience have also been generally supportive, although there are also some discordant notes. Thus, the Schlegel and DiTecco (1982) study described earlier obtained stronger attitude–behavior correlations among high-school students with relatively little direct experience concerning the use of marijuana than among students with a great deal of direct experience. Finally, there is some evidence that the attitude's internal consistency can have an effect on its relation to specific actions, but this effect has not always been obtained.

*An integrative framework: accessibility*

If there is one overriding problem with this approach to improving correlations between general dispositions and specific behaviors it is the multitude of secondary characteristics that have been identified. However, recent work by Fazio and his associates (Fazio, 1986; Fazio and Williams, 1986; Fazio *et al.*, 1982; Sherman and Fazio, 1983) promises to provide an integrative theoretical framework in this domain. These theorists have advanced a process model of the way attitudes guide behavior. According to the model, accessibility of attitude in memory is perhaps the prime moderator of the attitude–behavior relation. An attitude is thought to be highly accessible if there is a strong association between the attitude object and an evaluative response. This associative strength is defined operationally as the time it takes to react to questions about the attitude object: the smaller this response latency, the more accessible in memory the attitude is assumed to be. Attitude accessibility is said to determine the extent to which an attitude is activated upon exposure to the attitude object, and hence the extent to which the attitude is likely to guide behavior in the presence of the object. It follows that attitude–behavior consistency should increase with attitude accessibility.

The idea that accessibility or salience of an attitude can affect its relation to behavior is not completely original. Brown (1974) demonstrated the moderating effect of attitudinal salience in a study of compliance with the law. High-school students completed several multi-item scales designed to assess attitudes toward the law in general, toward the federal laws of the United States, toward the police, and toward the courts. The salience of these attitudes was assessed by asking the respondents how often they thought about the law in general and about the unlawfulness of such activities as crossing a street against a red light, littering in public places, and speeding in an automobile. Scores on this measure were used to divide participants into low, moderate, and high salience subgroups. A scale based on self-reports of compliance with the law on such matters as shoplifting, traffic regulations, and the use of narcotics served as the measure of behavior. Consistent with expectations, attitude–behavior correlations were relatively weak when attitudinal salience was low ($r = 0.18–0.33$); they increased in magnitude for respondents whose attitudes were moderately salient ($r = 0.32 –0.45$); and they were strongest in the high salience subgroup ($r = 0.42–0.65$).

The results of research concerning the moderating effects of direct experience, involvement and confidence can be reinterpreted in the light of the salience or accessibility notion. Thus, it is now argued that direct experience with an attitude object, involvement in the attitudinal domain, and confidence in an expressed attitude all increase the attitude's accessibility in memory (see Fazio, 1986; Fazio and Williams, 1986; Sherman and Fazio, 1983). As a result, the attitude is more likely to be activated and to guide behavior under these conditions. In partial support of this claim, it has been found that, in comparison to second-hand information, direct experience with intellectual puzzles leads to the formation of attitudes that are more accessible from memory (Fazio *et al.*, 1982, 1983).

Fazio and Williams (1986) provided more direct evidence for the link between attitude accessibility and the attitude–behavior relation. Voters in the 1984 United States presidential election were interviewed several months prior to the election. Among other things, they were asked to express their attitudes toward the two major candidates, Reagan and Mondale, on a 5-point scale, and the latencies of their responses were recorded. On the basis of these response latencies, participants were divided into high- and low-accessibility subgroups. Immediately following the election, participants were contacted by telephone and were asked to report whether they had voted in the election and, if so, for whom they had voted. As in previous studies of voting behavior (see Campbell *et al.*, 1960; Fishbein and Ajzen, 1981), the correlation between attitudes toward the candidates and voting choice was quite high. However, in accordance with expectations, this correlation was significantly stronger among voters who had relatively easy access to their attitudes ($r = 0.88$) than among voters whose attitudes were less accessible ($r = 0.72$).

*Situational factors as moderators*

While most efforts to identify moderating variables have been directed at individual differences and at a disposition's secondary characteristics, several potential candidates of a situational nature have also been investigated. The general idea here is that different indicators of the same disposition will be more consistent with each other in some situations than in others.

An obvious potential moderating variable related to the behavioral context is *situational constraint*. On the basis of self-ratings, Monson *et al.* (1982) selected extraverted and introverted college students for participation in their study. Each student's taped interaction with two confederates was rated for the amount spoken and the degree of extraversion displayed. To manipulate situational constraint, the two confederates either acted neutrally during the interaction, thus permitting expression of the student's personality trait, or they constrained the student's behavior by strongly encouraging or discouraging talking on his part. As might be expected, there was significantly less behavioral variance in the two high constraint conditions than in the condition of low constraint. That is, students tended to talk when they were encouraged to do so and to be relatively quiet when they were discouraged from talking. There was much greater variability in behavior when the confederates acted neutrally. The correlations between extraversion–introversion and behavior showed the expected pattern: stronger correlations ($r = 0.56$ and $0.63$ for the two measures of behavior) under low constraint than under high constraint ($r = 0.10$ and $0.38$).

Warner and DeFleur (1969), however, reported moderating effects of the situation that appear to be at variance with these findings. A large sample of college students was divided at the median score on a scale designed to assess attitudes toward Blacks. The measure of behavior was each participant's signed indication of willingness or refusal to perform one of eight behaviors, ranging from making a small donation to a charity for Black students to dating an attractive Black student. These commitments were elicited by means of a letter sent to each participant. For half the sample the letter assured anonymity of response, whereas for the other half it indicated that the participant's response would be made public in campus newspapers. It stands to reason that the public condition involved greater social constraints than did the private condition. We might thus expect behavior to be more consistent with attitudes in the latter than in the former. Although the results of the study must be interpreted with caution because of a very low response rate, they showed exactly the opposite pattern. The effect of attitude on signed approval or disapproval of the requested behavior was greater in the public condition (a difference of 77.8% between respondents with positive and negative attitudes toward Blacks) than in the private condition (a difference of 17.2%).

Another situational moderator that has been investigated is much more subtle in nature. Instead of assessing existing individual differences in private self-consciousness, it is possible to manipulate the situation such as to create high or low levels of *self-awareness*. Wicklund and his associates (Wicklund, 1975; Duval and Wicklund, 1972) have done this in the laboratory, typically by means of confronting the participant with a mirror. Like private self-consciousness, heightened self-awareness is expected to increase consistency between general dispositions and specific actions.

To test this hypothesis, Carver (1975) performed two replications of a study in which attitudes toward punishment were assessed by means of several questions concerning its perceived effectiveness and the participant's willingness to use punishment. At a later point in time, the participants had an opportunity to administer shocks of varying intensities on 35 "error" trials in the Buss (1961) aggression paradigm described earlier. Depending on experimental conditions, a mirror was either present or absent during shock administration. In the first study, the two attitude measures predicted mean shock levels with correlations of 0.57 and 0.58 when the mirror was present but the correlations were close to zero when the mirror was absent. A significant interaction between attitude and presence of mirror was also found in the second study, but no correlations were reported.

Similar results were obtained by Pryor *et al.* (1977) with respect to the relation between personality and overt behavior. A mirror was either present or absent during administration of a questionnaire designed to assess sociability. Several days later, the male participants were observed interacting with a female confederate who assumed a passive role. The behavioral measure of sociability was a combination of the number of words emitted by the participant and the confederate's rating of his sociability. There were again two replications of the study, with trait–behavior correlations of 0.55 and 0.73 in the mirror condition and 0.03 and 0.28 in the condition without a mirror.[2]

One final factor related to the situation is its *competency requirements* (Mischel, 1984). This factor is actually a combination of situational and personal variables. Mischel (1983, 1984) has argued that consistency of behavior across situations may often be reflective of rigidity, maladjustment, and an inability to cope adequately with the requirements of a given situation. Whenever the competency requirements of the situation exceed the level of competence possessed by the individual, behavior will tend to follow well-established patterns. Mischel thus hypothesized that we will find greater consistency in behavior under such conditions. A study conducted by Wright (1983) was designed to test this hypothesis (see Mischel, 1984). Emotionally disturbed children in summer camps served as subjects. Behaviors reflecting aggressiveness and withdrawal were of particular interest. Judges rated the situations in which behaviors were observed in terms of their cognitive and self-regulatory requirements, and they also rated the competencies of each child to meet those requirements. Within each behavioral category, correlations were computed among the various specific behaviors involved. These correlations were reported for two replications of the study. When the children's competencies were up to the requirements of the situation, the mean correlations (across behaviors and replications) were 0.35 for aggression and 0.17 for withdrawal. In contrast, when the situational requirements exceeded the competencies of the children, the corresponding correlations were 0.67 and 0.53.

In conclusion, despite the frequent assertion that personal and situational factors interact to produce behavior, relatively few studies seem to have submitted this hypothesis to a direct test. The prime situational candidate for an interaction effect, situational constraint, has produced inconclusive results. The experiment by Monson *et al.* (1982) created conditions that virtually guaranteed that the sociability trait would find expression only under low situational constraints. Manipulating constraints in a less blatant fashion, Warner and DeFleur (1969) reported results that appear inconsistent with the original interaction hypothesis. It is worth noting, however, that their results can be explained by reference to impression management theory (Tedeschi *et al.*, 1971). According to this theory, people strive to maintain the appearance of consistency between their attitudes and their behaviors in order to create a favorable impression on others. This tendency should, of course, be stronger when the behavior is performed in public rather than in private. Warner and DeFleur's finding that general attitudes toward Blacks were better predictors of specific behaviors under public as compared to private conditions is quite consistent with this impression management approach. As to the moderating effects of a situation's competency requirements, an initial study yielded some promising findings but more research is needed to demonstrate their replicability in other settings.

## Behavioral factors as moderators

The final source of variance in behavioral consistency to be considered has to do with the particular action that is taken as an indicator of an underlying disposition. The predictive validity of an attitude or a personality trait may be greater for some behaviors than for others. The question is how we can identify behaviors that are *relevant* for a given disposition and distinguish them from behaviors that are less relevant. One possible approach, taken by Buss and Craik (1980, 1981), is described in Chapter 3. These investigators examined the relevance of a behavior to a given disposition (e.g. dominance) by asking a sample of judges to rate how good an example of the disposition it was. However, rather than looking at the correlations between the disposition and each individual behavior in the light of these ratings, Buss and Craik divided the total set of behaviors into four relevance categories (from low to high) and showed that predictive validity increased with the rated relevance of the actions comprising a multiple-act index.

By way of contrast, Fishbein and Ajzen (1974) reported data on the prediction of individual behaviors varying in their rated relevance to a disposition. It will be recalled (see p. 54) that in this study attitudes toward religion were assessed by means of four standard scales and that the college students who participated in the study indicated whether or not they had performed each of 100 behaviors related to matters of religion. An independent group of judges rated, for each behavior, the likelihood that it would be performed by individuals with positive attitudes toward religion and the likelihood that it would be performed by individuals with negative attitudes toward religion. The absolute difference between these two conditional probabilities was used as a measure of the behavior's relevance to the attitude. This measure of relevance was then compared with the correlation between each behavior and the attitude score. The results thus show the extent to which the correlation between general attitudes and a specific action can be predicted from the action's judged relevance. These predictions ranged from 0.40 to 0.47 across the four measures of attitude toward religion.

As mentioned in Chapter 3, Sjöberg (1982) replicated the Fishbein and Ajzen (1974) procedures in the domain of attitudes and behaviors with respect to aid to developing countries. In his study, the prediction of attitude–behavior correlations from the behavior's judged relevance to the attitude was 0.28 and 0.36 for two measures of attitude. Sjöberg also demonstrated the utility of a somewhat simpler procedure to identify the relevance of a given behavior, namely, by using the correlation between the specific action and the total behavioral score. This index of a behavior's representativeness of the behavioral domain predicted attitude–behavior correlations at the level of 0.48 and 0.45 for the two measures of attitude.

## Moderating variables and the question of consistency

There is an intuitive appeal to the moderating variables approach to the consistency problem. After all, it seems reasonable to argue that some conditions are more conducive than others to a strong association between general dispositions and specific actions. And, indeed, the various moderating variables that have been proposed give us a general sense of some of the conditions under which we can or cannot expect consistency between general attitudes or personality traits on the one hand and specific behaviors on the other. However, the picture that emerges is far from clear.

At least two factors greatly complicate the search for moderating variables. First, the number of variables that might moderate the relation between general dispositions and specific actions is potentially unlimited. A study by Drake and Sobrero (1985) illustrates some unconventional possibilities. Correlations between private self-consciousness and attributions of responsibility to the self, as well as correlations between attitudes toward affirmative action and a hiring decision, were found to be moderated by whether instructions over earphones were given to the left or to the right ear. These correlations were much stronger when instructions were given to the right ear (thereby presumably activating the left cerebral hemisphere) than when they were given to the left ear. Clearly, without a conceptual framework for guidance, any attempt to identify all important moderators is bound to be a frustrating experience. The steady accumulation of additional moderators over the past few years, and the recurrent failure to replicate earlier findings regarding the effects of a given moderator, may be the harbingers of things to come.

Moreover, it should also be remembered that the discovery of a factor that moderates attitude–behavior or trait–behavior relations is very much a mixed blessing. "Though predictions are improved for one subgroup, there remains usually another subgroup for whom predictive efficiency is diminished" (Zedeck, 1971, p. 307). Thus, we may be able to predict, say, tardiness on the job from a personality measure of conscientiousness for employees who are highly self-conscious, but what do we do with employees who possess only a moderate or low degree of this characteristic? Clearly, it would be preferable if general conscientiousness could predict punctuality on the job for all employees. Unfortunately, the evidence reviewed in Chapter 2 shows that correlations between general dispositions and specific actions of this kind tend to be very low.

The second complicating factor in the contingent consistency approach is the possibility – indeed the likelihood – that the moderating effects of one variable will be found to depend on still other moderators. That is, we can expect higher-order interactions to obscure any systematic lower-order interactions between dispositions and identified moderating factors. Several recent studies have already demonstrated this problem. Zanna *et al.* (1980) showed that the self-monitoring tendency affected attitude–behavior correlations in the expected manner only for certain individuals. These investigators used a self-report of religiosity to predict several measures of religious behavior: a multiple-act index based on 90 self-reported behaviors of a religious nature, an index based on the number of times participants had attended religious services and prayed in private, and an index based on the number of times they had been intoxicated with alcohol and had used illegal drugs. No significant differences were observed in the attitude–behavior correlations of low and high self-monitoring individuals. However, to complicate matters, the study demonstrated a significant second-order interaction such that attitude–behavior correlations depended on a particular combination of self-monitoring tendency and self-reported behavioral variability. Correlations were highest for low self-monitoring individuals who reported that their religious behavior was relatively invariant across situations. All other combinations of self-monitoring and variability resulted in lower correlations of about equal magnitude.

Snyder and Kendzierski (1982) also reported second-order interactions involving the self-monitoring variable. This study again employed Snyder and Swann's (1976) hypothetical sex discrimination case. With neutral instructions, namely to weigh all relevant evidence before rendering a verdict, the study failed to replicate the original findings; that is, there was no significant difference between low and high self-monitoring individuals in terms of the correlation between attitudes toward affirmative action and the nature of the verdict ($r = 0.18$ and $-0.17$, respectively). The expected difference emerged, however, when attitudes were made salient or "available" by asking participants to think about their attitudes toward affirmative action before the court case was presented. In this condition of the experiment, the attitude–behavior correlation for low self-monitoring individuals was $0.47$, but for high self-monitors it was only $0.18$. Finally, attitudes predicted verdicts about equally well for both types of participants ($r = 0.45$ and $0.60$) in a third condition which encouraged participants to think about the implications of their verdicts prior to rendering them but after having read the court case.

Another example of qualifications that must be put on the effects of moderating variables can be found in two studies on the relationship between attitudes toward punishment and mean shock level administered in the Buss (1961) learning paradigm (Froming et al., 1982). The moderating variable of interest in these studies was self-awareness. According to Duval and Wicklund (1972) it should make no difference how self-awareness is brought about, whether by means of a mirror, a TV camera, or an audience. Heightened self-awareness should improve dispositional prediction of behavior, no matter how it is created. However, Froming et al. showed that manipulation of self-awareness via a mirror and via the presence of an audience can produce very different effects. Moreover, the moderating effects were also found to depend on the type of audience. At the beginning of the term, college students completed a 9-item attitude scale toward punishment, once expressing their own opinions and again for the views most people have on the issue. In the first study, the respondents selected for participation had more negative attitudes toward punishment than the attitudes they attributed to others, whereas the reverse was true in the second study. Shocks on 20 "error" trials were administered without a mirror (control condition), in the presence of a mirror, or in the presence of a two-person audience. In the first study, the audience was said either merely to observe the subject or to evaluate his/her effectiveness as a teacher; in the second study, the audience consisted either of advanced psychology students (experts) or of classmates. As in previous research, the presence of a mirror was found to produce behavior more in accordance with personal attitudes toward punishment, but the presence of an evaluative or expert audience induced behavior in accordance not with personal attitudes but with perceived social norms. The nonevaluative and nonexpert audiences had no significant effects on attitude–behavior correspondence. The investigators explained the observed differences between mirror and effective audience conditions by means of Carver and Scheier's (1981) distinction between *private* and *public* self-consciousness. Different environmental cues are assumed to evoke different types on self-consciousness. Specifically, the presence of a mirror is assumed to produce private self-consciousness, whereas an evaluative audience is said to evoke public self-consciousness. The results of the study are quite consistent with this idea.

Whatever interpretations we manage to offer for higher-order interactions, there is no question that they greatly complicate the picture. As Cronbach (1975) has noted,

> Once we attend to interactions, we enter a hall of mirrors that extends to infinity. However far we carry our analysis – to third order or fifth order or any other – untested interactions of a still higher order can be envisioned (p. 119).

Speaking out against the search for person–situation interactions, Nisbett (1977, p. 235) made the following observations:

> There are serious inherent disadvantages to interaction hypotheses, notably the difficulty of disconfirming them, their illusory aura of precision, and the disadvantages of complex designs employed to test them.

Beyond pointing to the inherent difficulties of such an approach, these observations raise another troubling issue: whenever an investigation fails to support a hypothesized moderating effect of a given variable, rather than rejecting the hypothesis, we can attribute the failure to as yet undiscovered additional factors upon which the effect of our moderating variable may be contingent in the sense of a higher-order interaction.

However, let us assume for a moment that our research efforts did result in the replicable identification of the many moderating factors and their higher-order interactions. Even in such an ideal world we would still be left with a serious problem as far as the prediction of specific actions from general dispositions is concerned. A successful moderating variables approach leads ultimately to the unavoidable conclusion that general dispositions are, by and large, poor predictors of specific action; they can be expected to predict only some behaviors, for some individuals, in some situations.

Theoretically, any single instance of behavior can be

> predicted if all the right moderator variables are included. This is no more than to say that behavior is determined, and that if we knew everything that determined it, we could predict it. However, to do so might require the addition of so many moderator variables that they would generate interactions of such complexity as to make the procedure unfeasible and the results uninterpretable (Epstein, 1983b, p. 377).

Although we may be able to create in the laboratory the unique set of circumstances required for consistency, the particular combination of factors required is unlikely to obtain under natural conditions. The general lack of consistency between global dispositional measures and specific actions documented in Chapter 2 attests to the fact that in most cases, the prevailing conditions are far from optimal.

## Summary and conclusions

The moderating variables approach to the consistency dilemma has provided some useful insights into the relation between general dispositions and specific actions. Strong relations of this kind have been found to depend on a variety of factors that have to do with individual differences among people, secondary characteristics of the disposition, aspects of the situation, and the nature of the behavior. The moderating effects of some of these variables are better understood than those of others. The present chapter reviews a considerable number of empirical investigations in some detail. This is done in an effort to show some of the difficulties and complexities involved in the search for contingency effects.

With the exception of an attitude's internal consistency, such secondary characteristics of attitude as the confidence with which it is held, the amount of information on which it is based, involvement with the attitude object, and the way in which the attitude is acquired, all seem to have a systematic impact on the accuracy of behavioral prediction. Moreover, the trend toward constructing an ever-increasing list of secondary moderating characteristics of attitudes is being overtaken by work on the processes whereby attitudes

guide behavior (Fazio, 1986; Fazio *et al.*, 1982, 1983). The focus on attitude accessibility reduces the number of contingencies that need to be considered and provides an integrative theoretical framework that can help explain how secondary attitude characteristics, and perhaps other variables as well, exert their moderating effects.

In contrast, research on such individual difference variables as self-monitoring, private self-consciousness, and the tendency to be consistent in a given behavioral domain, has produced rather mixed results. Although it appears that these factors can have a moderating influence on the relation between verbal measures of global dispositions and specific behaviors of a nonverbal kind, obtained effects have not always been replicated and higher-order interactions involving these variables have been reported.

As to situation-by-disposition interactions, relatively few studies have examined this issue directly in relation to the prediction of behavior. Although it seems clear that features of the situation are likely to interact in complex ways with general personality traits and attitudes, we have as yet little information about the kinds of situations in which stable dispositions can be expected to guide behavior. A natural candidate, situational constraints, has thus far produced inconclusive results.

Finally, several studies have shown that general attitudes and personality traits are better predictors of some specific behaviors than of others. However, this research has been of a largely descriptive nature. Although we can identify behaviors that are more or less likely to correlate with general dispositions, we do not know as yet why one behavior can be predicted with greater accuracy than another.

Despite the great efforts invested in the search for moderating variables, and despite the progress that has been made, this approach is unlikely to open the way to dispositional prediction of specific actions. Several interrelated problems lead us to reach this conclusion. While identifying some subset of individuals, situations, dispositions, or behaviors for which prediction is possible, discovery of a moderating variable at the same time also identifies another subset for which prediction is not possible. As the number of known moderators increases, and as these moderators are found to interact with still other variables, the latter subset increases at the expense of the former. From a theoretical point of view, identification of additional moderating factors can enhance our understanding of psychological processes involved in going from dispositions to actions, but from a practical point of view, the contribution of this approach is more questionable. The next two chapters therefore present and discuss an alternative approach to the dispositional prediction of specific actions.

## Notes

1. Most tests of moderating effects unfortunately use the procedure of comparing subgroups that differ in terms of the moderating variable. This is not an optimal analytic strategy as it tends to have low statistical power (Cohen, 1983) and may confound differences between the subgroup variances with true moderator effects (Baron and Kenny, 1986; Tellegen *et al.*, 1982). A preferable approach is to use hierarchical regression analysis to test for interactions between independent and moderator variables (Cohen, 1978).
2. Note that in this study the mirror was present or absent during the administration of the questionnaire, whereas in the Carver (1975) study the self-awareness manipulation was effected during performance of the behavior.

## Suggestions for further readings

1. Snyder, M. (1982). When believing means doing: Creating links between attitudes and behavior. In M. P. Zanna, E. T. Higgins and C. P. Herman (Eds), *Consistency in social behavior: The Ontario symposium*, Vol. 2, pp. 105–30. Hillsdale, NJ: Lawrence Erlbaum Associates. This chapter reviews the role of the self-monitoring tendency as a moderator of the attitude–behavior relation.
2. Fazio, R. H. and Zanna, M. P. (1981). Direct experience and attitude-behavior consistency. In L. Berkowitz (Ed.), *Advances in experimental social psychology*, Vol. 14, pp. 161–202. San Diego: Academic Press. This chapter illustrates the moderating effects of such secondary characteristics of an attitude as direct experience and confidence.
3. Sherman, S. J. and Fazio, R. H. (1983). Parallels between attitudes and traits as predictors of behavior. *Journal of Personality*, 51, 308–45. In this article, the authors review the effects of various moderating variables on the relation between attitudes and behavior and between personality traits and behavior.
4. Cronbach, L. J. (1975). Beyond the two disciplines of scientific psychology. *American Psychologist*, 30, 116–27. This article presents a sophisticated discussion of some of the problems inherent in the interactionist (or moderating variables) approach to the prediction of behavior.

# 5 / THE PRINCIPLE OF COMPATIBILITY

> Common sense, which, one would say, means the shortest
> line between two points.
>
> *Emerson*

At first glance the intuitive logic that links a general attitude or
personality trait to a specific behavior appears unassailable. After all,
it seems reasonable to expect, for example, that people who hold
favorable attitudes toward communism are more likely to subscribe
to a communist newspaper than are people who hold unfavorable
attitudes toward communism. Likewise, it would appear that in
comparison to egotistic individuals, altruists should be more likely to
donate money to a fund for the needy or to help an old lady across the
street. On closer examination, however, the matter turns out to be
more complicated than it appears at first. The difficulty has to do
with the way in which we specify behavioral implications of a given
attitude or personality trait. To see why this poses a problem, let us
examine some absurd possibilities. Consider, for example, an investigation conducted in France which tests the relation between attitudes toward the People's Republic of China and the number of
hamburgers eaten at the Burger King restaurant on the Champs
Élysées in Paris. One would have to go through considerable mental
contortions to explain why attitudes should be linked to behavior in
this particular case, and the results of the empirical research would
almost certainly be disappointing. However, what if we tried to
relate attitudes toward the People's Republic of China to voting for
the communist candidate in the French national elections? Now it
might appear that a correlation should emerge. Or, in the domain of
personality, imagine a study that examines the relation between
dominance and the number of times a person walks to work instead
of taking the bus. Here again we would expect little predictive
validity, but if we substituted energy level for dominance, a strong

relation might appear plausible. It can be seen that a given behavior is considered consistent or inconsistent with a person's attitude or personality trait on the basis of largely intuitive considerations. It follows that, in the absence of a more formal and explicit way of deciding whether or not a given behavior is implied by an attitude or personality trait, many tests of attitude–behavior or trait–behavior relations are little more than tests of the investigator's intuition. From a theoretical point of view they are of rather limited value.

We have seen in previous chapters that dispositional prediction of specific behaviors has proved to be a recalcitrant problem. Global attitudes and personality traits are largely unrelated to particular actions; aggregation of specific behaviors into multiple-act indices demonstrates the utility of broad dispositions but adds little to our understanding of the factors that determine a *given* behavior; and the search for moderating variables ultimately leads to a dead end in that it restricts the predictive validity of global dispositional measures to a small subset of behaviors, individuals, and situations. Some of these problems are perhaps inevitable in the light of the above observations regarding the intuitive procedures whereby attitudes or traits are considered relevant for specific actions. In the present chapter we will see that it is, after all, possible to predict specific actions from behavioral dispositions, but that doing so requires going beyond intuition to decide what kinds of attitudes or traits should correlate with a particular behavior. The approach to be described reconceptualizes the nature of behavioral dispositions by turning to attitudes and personality traits that, by their very nature, are closely tied to specific behavioral tendencies.

## Generality of behavioral dispositions

As we have noted repeatedly, attitudes and personality traits are usually conceptualized as relatively stable dispositions that exert pervasive influence on a broad range of behaviors. In the case of attitudes, the disposition is of an evaluative nature and the behaviors guided by it are directed at the attitude object. Personality traits, on the other hand, are defined in terms of a general class or category of actions that reflect the influence of the same disposition. Yet it is not clear at all how general a trait or attitude must be for it to be considered a behavioral disposition. Chapter 1 shows that empirical research has identified five broad personality dimensions:

extraversion, agreeableness, conscientiousness, emotional stability, and culturedness. However, each of these dimensions is composed of more narrowly defined personality characteristics, such as talkativeness and caution in the case of extraversion–introversion and tidiness and perseverance in the case of conscientiousness. Perhaps it is possible to reduce a trait's generality still further, thus moving the disposition closer to the behavior that is to be predicted. In a similar vein, the object of an attitude is not necessarily a person, group, institution, or policy; it can also be defined in terms of a particular behavior. People hold attitudes not only toward religion but also toward praying in private; toward democracy and toward voting in a given election; toward doctors and toward maintaining a medical regimen. In fact, the standard measurement procedures described in Chapter 1 have been used to assess not only very general attitudes but also attitudes toward such specific behaviors as smoking marijuana (Schlegel, 1975), using birth control methods (Kothandapani, 1971), drinking alcohol (Veevers, 1971), and so on.

## Target, action, context, and time

The above discussion suggests that the behavioral disposition defined by an attitude or personality trait can vary along a dimension of generality, from the very broad and all-inclusive to the specific. The following analysis defines the dimension of generality in a more systematic fashion. Any measure of a behavioral disposition, whether verbal or nonverbal, can be defined in terms of four elements: the target at which the disposition is directed, the particular action or actions involved, the context in which the action occurs, and the time of its occurrence (see Ajzen and Fishbein, 1977; Fishbein and Ajzen, 1975). The generality or specificity of each element depends on the measurement procedures employed. A single observation of an action is a highly specific behavioral indicator in that it involves a given behavior, directed at a particular target, and performed in a given context and at a given point in time. By way of contrast, measures of global attitudes toward objects and generalized personality traits specify no particular action, i.e. they are very broadly defined in terms of the action element. Table 5.1 illustrates different levels of generality with respect to the disposition to behave in a sociable manner. Examination of the table shows that we can move from a lower level of generality to a higher level by aggregating

*Table 5.1* Levels of generality

| Global | | Disposition to be sociable | | |
|---|---|---|---|---|
| *Behavioral tendency* | Attend parties | Talk to friends | Reveal private feelings | Ask for help |
| *Specific context* | Attend parties at place of work | Talk to friends by phone | Reveal private feelings to strangers | Ask for help from coworkers |
| *Specific context and time* | Attend party at place of work on a given weekend | Phone friends next Sunday | Reveal private feelings to strangers on birthday | Ask for help from coworkers on a night shift |

across one or more elements. Thus, if we record the number of times a person talks to friends on the phone, rather than observing this behavior only next Sunday, we generalize across the time element and obtain a measure of the tendency to talk with friends in a certain context (on the telephone). If we go one step further and record all occasions on which a person talks to friends, rather than merely telephone conversations, we also generalize across the contextual element and thus derive a measure of the general tendency to talk with friends. Finally, as shown in Chapter 3, by aggregating over the different behavioral tendencies (talking to friends, attending parties, revealing private feelings, etc.), we reach the highest level of generality, namely the level of the disposition to be sociable.

Returning to the dispositional prediction of specific actions, it is mentioned in Chapter 3 that we are rarely interested in the lowest level of generality that involves a unique context and specific point in time. As a general rule, we are more concerned with predicting and understanding behavioral tendencies or regularities across occasions. Thus, we may want to predict and explain safe driving over a period of time, rather than on a given afternoon; or we may be interested in the tendency, over time, to discipline children by means of corporal punishment. In behavioral tendencies of this kind, the target and action elements are constant, the context is also relatively stable from one occasion to another in the sense that it is appropriate for the behavior to occur, but the time element is broadly generalized. When referring to dispositional prediction of specific behaviors in the following discussions, we will have in mind these behavioral tendencies over time.

## The principle of compatibility

In their review of research on the attitude–behavior relation, Ajzen and Fishbein (1977) formulated a "principle of compatibility" that can be stated as follows: two indicators of a given disposition are said to be *compatible* with each other to the extent that their target, action, context, and time elements are assessed at identical levels of generality or specificity. Further, consistency between two indicators of a disposition is a function of the degree to which the indicators are, in this sense, compatible with each other. Thus, according to the principle of compatibility, the more similar the target, action, context, and time elements of one indicator to those of the other, the stronger the statistical relation between them.

The principle of compatibility is very similar to the contiguity hypothesis in Guttman's (1955, 1957, 1959) facet theory. Guttman proposed that any variable can be analyzed in terms of an underlying facet structure. The action, target, context, and time elements of behavioral dispositions are examples of facets, and their levels of generality constitute facet elements. Like the principle of compatibility, "The contiguity hypothesis of facet theory states that the correlation between two variables increases with the similarity between the facet elements defining them" (Guttman, 1957, p. 130; see also Foa, 1958; Olweus, 1980).

Weigel *et al.* (1974) demonstrated the importance of compatibility between the *target* element of the attitude measure and the target at which the behavior is directed. Residents of a community in the western United States participated in this investigation which was conducted with the assistance of the local chapter of the Sierra Club, an organization dedicated to such issues as conservation of natural resources and pollution control. Five months following administration of an initial attitude survey, participants were asked to commit themselves to various activities involving the Sierra Club. Their degree of compliance or refusal was used to compute a 4-step behavioral scale. The lowest level on the scale consisted of refusing to have any further contact with the Sierra Club and the remaining three levels ranged from agreeing to be on the club's mailing list to becoming a club member. It can be seen that this behavioral measure has the Sierra Club as its target and that it represents a generalization across different actions.

Four attitudes, varying in their degree of compatibility with the behavior, were assessed in the initial survey: attitudes toward the Sierra Club, toward conservation of natural resources, toward pollution control, and toward a pure environment in general. Clearly, the target element of the first attitude measure was the same as the target element of the behavior (the Sierra Club). The target elements of the next two attitudes, although not the same as that of the behavior, were issues of importance to the Sierra Club, i.e. conservation of natural resources and pollution control. Finally, the target element of attitude toward environmental protection in general had the lowest degree of compatibility with the target element of the behavior.

The results of the investigation were quite consistent with the principle of compatibility. As the degree of compatibility between target elements decreased, so did the attitude–behavior correlation. The behavioral criterion had a correlation of 0.60 with attitudes toward the Sierra Club (high compatibility), correlations of 0.37 and 0.38 with attitudes toward conservation and pollution control (moderate compatibility), and a nonsignificant correlation of 0.16 with attitudes toward a pure environment (low compatibility).

The operation of the compatibility principle has also been demonstrated by experimentally manipulating the similarity between the target elements of attitudes and actions (Lord *et al.*, 1984). In the first of two studies, college students at Princeton University reported their stereotypes of members of a certain "eating club" (fraternity or sorority) at the university by rating them on a set of 20 personality trait terms. At a later session, the participants expressed their attitudes toward members of the club and toward working with a member of the club on a joint project. They were then given paragraph descriptions of two persons they could work with, one description conforming closely to the individual's stereotype of club members, the other much less in accordance with the stereotype. Finally, the participants rated how much they would like to work with each of the two club members. The target element of this behavioral preference measure is the particular person described in the paragraph. This target is clearly more similar to the target of the attitude measures (members of the club in general) when the person described conforms to the respondent's stereotype of club members than when it does not. Consistent with the principle of compatibility, the correlations between the two attitude measures and the behavioral preference were stronger under high compatibility in target elements ($r = 0.49$ and $0.69$) than under low compatibility ($r = 0.27$ and $0.32$). Similar results were obtained in a second study dealing with the relation between attitudes toward homosexuals and the willingness to visit a homosexual individual who was described in accordance with, or not in accordance with, the respondent's stereotype of homosexuals.

In this chapter, however, we are interested less in compatibility between the target elements of two dispositional measures than in compatibility between their *action* elements. According to the principle of compatibility, we should be able to predict behavior at any level of generality or specificity, so long as the predictor is equally general or specific, i.e. so long as the two measures involve not only the same target, but also the same action, context, and time elements. The principle of aggregation discussed in Chapter 3 can be recognized as a special case of the compatibility principle. It represents the case of compatibility at relatively high levels of generality. By aggregating over a set of occasions we obtain measures of behavioral trends that correspond in their level of generality to other measures of the same behavioral trends obtained by aggregating over a different set of occasions. Of greater interest, when we aggregate across different behaviors in a given domain or directed at a given object, the resulting multiple-act index corresponds in its level of generality to a properly constructed measure of a general personality trait or attitude. As suggested by the principle of compatibility, aggregated measures of behavior are indeed found to exhibit consistency with each other and to correlate well with questionnaire measures of general attitudes and personality traits (see Chapter 3). By the same reasoning, the principle of compatibility offers a promising avenue to the dispositional prediction of specific action tendencies. According to the principle, we must measure the predictor such that it reflects the specific response tendency of interest. This possibility is examined below, first with respect to personality traits and then with respect to attitudes.

## Personality traits and specific response tendencies

We can reduce personality traits to the level of specific response tendencies in a number of different ways. If the principle of compatibility is upheld, behavior-specific trait measures will correlate well with the corresponding action tendencies.

*Temporal stability of response tendencies*

It is often proposed that the best predictor of future behavior is performance or nonperformance of the same behavior in the past. In other words, if a person is known to have exhibited a tendency to perform a given behavior, we can assume that, barring unforeseen events, the tendency will continue. Thus, in a random sample of respondents, cigarette smoking in the foreseeable future can be predicted with a high degree of accuracy if we know whether a person has or has not been smoking in the past. Temporal stability of behavioral tendencies will be greater for some behaviors than for others, and it will vary with the amount of time covered in the prediction. The greater the time interval, the more likely it is that intervening events will modify the behavioral tendency. Participation in a smoking cessation program, for example, may reduce or eliminate cigarette consumption in some smokers, while previous nonsmokers may take up use of tobacco in the same time period. Nevertheless, in many instances we would expect sufficient temporal stability to permit fairly accurate prediction from past to future behavior.

A few concrete illustrations may be helpful. In a laboratory experiment, Locke *et al.* (1984) examined students' task performance over a series of trials. The task involved finding uses for common objects, such as bricks or clothes hangers, and the measure of behavior was the number of distinct uses listed by a participant. After some initial training, performance on trials 5 and 6 was predicted from performance on trial 4. The correlation between prior and later behavior in this situation was found to be 0.68. Ajzen and Madden (1986) reported a significant correlation of moderate magnitude between prior and later behavior. In this investigation, college students' class attendance was recorded on 16 consecutive occasions. The number of times students attended class on the first eight occasions was found to have a correlation of 0.46 with the number of times they attended class on the second eight occasions.

The studies by Locke *et al.* and by Ajzen and Madden involved a very short time-lag between prior and later behavior. The time-lag was much greater in other studies. For example, in their research on the American voter, Campbell *et al.* (1960) reported temporal stability of turnout in presidential elections. Respondents were asked to indicate, on a 4-point scale, how often they had voted in previous presidential elections and this measure of past behavior was used to predict voter turnout in the 1956 presidential election.[1] A secondary analysis of the Campbell *et al.* data reveals a correlation of 0.60. Similarly, consider use of marijuana among high-school students (Jessor and Jessor, 1977). On two occasions, separated by 1 year, the students in this study replied to four items that assessed the amount of marijuana they were using. Although the two observations of behavior were separated by a considerable period of time, the correlation between later and prior behavior was a respectable 0.53.

The above examples show that prior behavior can permit the accurate prediction of later behavior in many situations. Behavior can, however, also be quite variable over time. Some examples concerning temporal instability of behavioral trends can be found in Vinokur and Caplan's (1987; Vinokur *et al.*, 1987) research program on job-seeking behaviors of the unemployed. Obviously, job-seeking activities will tend to change once a person has found employment. However, even if we restrict the analysis to only those individuals who, over a period of time, fail to secure employment, we may find that their strategies of looking for a job have changed. In one of their studies, Vinokur and his associates assessed, at three points in time, the reported frequencies with which unemployed men performed each of ten job-seeking activities: read newspapers for job opportunities; checked with employment agencies; talked to friends, family or other people to get information about jobs; used or sent out a resumé to a prospective employer; registered for, or started, a job training program; filled out an application form for a job; telephoned, wrote, or visited potential employers; actually went for a job interview; did things to improve the impression they would make in a job interview (wore the right clothes, got a haircut, etc.); and phoned or went to their union's meeting place. The questionnaire assessing these behavioral tendencies was administered three times at 4-monthly intervals.

Table 5.2 shows the temporal stability or instability of the different behavioral tendencies.[2] Overall, there were clear individual differences in job-seeking behaviors that remained fairly stable over the time period investigated. The average correlation between initial behavioral reports and the reports provided 4 months later was 0.43; for the second 4-month period it was 0.40; and over the total 8-month period an average correlation of 0.33 was obtained.[3] Inspection of the individual behavioral tendencies, however, reveals considerable variation. The number of times people used their resumés, for example, and the number of times they went to their

*Table 5.2*   Temporal stability of job-seeking behaviors (Vinokur and Caplan, 1987)

|  | First 4 months | Second 4 months | 8 months |
|---|---|---|---|
| Read newspapers | 0.45 | 0.42 | 0.29 |
| Check with employment agencies | 0.38 | 0.31 | 0.34 |
| Talk to friends and others | 0.47 | 0.34 | 0.32 |
| Use or send out a resumé | 0.61 | 0.71 | 0.57 |
| Job training program | 0.20 | 0.43 | 0.03[a] |
| Apply for a job | 0.54 | 0.35 | 0.35 |
| Contact potential employers | 0.42 | 0.27 | 0.29 |
| Go for a job interview | 0.47 | 0.30 | 0.30 |
| Do things to improve appearance | 0.33 | 0.43 | 0.31 |
| Go to union | 0.51 | 0.56 | 0.54 |

[a] Not significant; all other correlations $P < 0.05$.

unions remained quite stable throughout. In contrast, checking with employment agencies and taking advantage of job training programs showed only modest degrees of temporal stability.

Clearly, then, behavioral tendencies can be quite stable over time, but they can also have rather low temporal stability when circumstances lead to modification of previous inclinations. A moment's reflection reveals, moreover, that even strong correlations between prior and later behavior are of little explanatory value. It is not very informative to say that people currently behave the way they do because they behaved that way in the past. We would still have to explain their past behavior as well as the reasons for the observed temporal stability in behavior. Most likely, temporal stability is the result of stability in the causal antecedents of the behavior under consideration. Certain factors will have led people to perform or not to perform the behavior in the past. To the extent that these factors persist over time, they will continue to exert their influence and thus produce the same behavior later on. If circumstances should change, the behavior will change as well and prior behavior will no longer predict later behavior. Only by identifying the causal antecedents of a behavior, and examining their vicissitudes over time, can we gain a proper understanding of the behavior's temporal stability (or instability).

*Self-reports and actual behavior*

In previous chapters we note that the relation between personality traits and behavior often revolves around compatibility between verbal responses and nonverbal responses in a given trait domain. When we consider dispositions at the level of individual behavioral tendencies, this question reduces to the validity of self-reports, i.e. to the correlation between two measures of a behavioral tendency: the tendency reported by the respondent versus that observed by independent means. Note that the issue here is not one of prediction, since both measures refer to behavior on the same set of occasions; rather, it is a question of the relation between what people say they do and what they actually do.

It is well known that self-reports may be biased by tendencies to report socially desirable behaviors and to deny performing socially undesirable behaviors (see Edwards, 1957). Such tendencies are especially likely in the case of "sensitive" behaviors, that is, behaviors that involve social stigmas or violations of the law. People may hesitate to admit that they have cheated on their income taxes or that they drive while intoxicated. Many attempts have been made over the years to develop measurement procedures that can circumvent these tendencies (e.g. Jones and Sigall, 1971; Warner, 1965). In this section, we briefly examine accuracy of self-reports for sensitive as opposed to nonsensitive behaviors.

With respect to sensitive behaviors, many studies have shown that people will tend to under-report performance of socially undesirable behaviors and over-report socially desirable behaviors. For example, Lamb and Stem (1978) reported that students tend to under-report the number of courses in which they received failing grades. In their sample of college students, the average number of courses with failing grades was 0.71, as indicated on students' records. However, when interviewed students admitted to having failed in only 0.46 courses on average, a significantly smaller number. Similarly, it has been found that high-school students tend to under-report their cigarette smoking (Bauman and Dent, 1982). When confronted with the knowledge that a physiological test of their actual smoking was being administered, a greater percentage of students admitted to having smoked cigarettes in the recent past than when not confronted with this information.[4] Interestingly, providing information about the physiological test had no effect on self-reports of cigarette smoking among the students' mothers. For the mothers, of course, this was not a particularly sensitive behavior since they were free to smoke or not to smoke as they wished. There was thus no reason for the mothers to under-report their smoking behavior.

When the behavior of interest is not particularly sensitive, self-reports tend to be quite accurate. For example, Pomazal and Jaccard (1976) telephoned college students and asked them to report whether or not they had donated blood during the previous week's campus blood drive. When compared with records of actual blood donations, these self-reports were found to be perfectly accurate. That is, all respondents who reported having donated blood were in fact on the official donor list, and those who reported that they had not given blood did not appear on the list. A high degree of self-report validity has also been substantiated in several other behavioral domains: participation in elections, possession of a library card, and possession of a driver's license (Parry and Crossley, 1950). The percentage of accurate reporting in these different domains varied from 60 to 98%.

In conclusion, when investigating a sensitive domain, respondents may – knowingly or unknowingly – misreport their behavior, but with respect to relatively insensitive behaviors, there is considerable consistency between self-reports and more objective measures. Even here, however, the utility of self-reports is severely limited. As noted above, they cannot be used to *predict* actual behavior because self-reports refer to prior behavior and are provided after the behavior has occurred. Moreover, as was true of prior behavior as a predictor of later behavior, self-reports have no explanatory value. We cannot meaningfully claim that a person performed a certain behavior because she said she performed it. Self-reports may reflect what actually happened, but they provide no explanation for it. We thus turn to a different kind of behavioral disposition that, even though tied to the specific response tendency, can still provide useful information about underlying psychological determinants of the behavior.

## Perceived behavioral control

Some personality dimensions may be considered dispositions to hold certain beliefs rather than dispositions to act in certain ways. Optimism, idealism, open-mindedness, etc., appear to fall into this category of traits. Perhaps the best-known case in point, however, is the concept of internal–external locus of control (Rotter, 1954, 1966). This concept refers to the generalized belief that one's outcomes are under the control of one's own behavior versus under the control of such external factors as powerful others or chance. Much research over the past 20 years has attempted to relate perceived locus of control to a broad range of specific actions (see Lefcourt, 1981a, 1982, 1983). In view of the poor predictive validity of other general personality traits documented in Chapter 2, it should come as no surprise that, by and large, the results have been disappointing. For example, early work with Rotter's (1966) internal–external (I–E) locus of control scale focused on achievement-related behavior. On the premise that internally oriented individuals are more likely to see a connection between their behavior and achievement than externally oriented individuals, it was hypothesized that the former would exert more effort and show greater persistence than the latter. However, investigations of the relation between locus of control beliefs and academic performance have often produced nonsignificant or inconclusive findings (see Warehime, 1972).

Another example is provided by the failure of general locus of control measures to predict social or political involvement. Believing that their actions can bring about desired goals, internals should be more likely to participate in the political process. However, as Levenson (1981, p. 49) stated in her review of this research, "Perhaps no area of study using the I–E construct has led to more confusing results than that of social and political activism." While some investigations obtained data in support of the hypothesis (e.g. Gore and Rotter, 1963), others found no differences between individuals with internal and external orientations (e.g. Evans and Alexander, 1970). Still other studies actually obtained results directly opposed to prediction, with externals showing greater involvement than internals (e.g. Sanger and Alker, 1972).

Results of this kind are not unexpected in the light of the principle of compatibility. Generalized locus of control beliefs are incompatible with specific behavioral tendencies in terms of target, action, and context; they can thus not be expected to permit accurate prediction. Rotter (1966) was quite aware of the need for more specialized measures of perceived locus of control. Although his I–E scale assesses generalized expectancies, his initial efforts were designed to develop a set of scales or subscales that would measure control expectations with regard to a number of different goal areas, such as achievement, social recognition, and affection (see Lefcourt, 1981b).

More specialized locus of control scales have indeed been constructed in subsequent years, most notably the Intellectual Achievement Responsibility (IAR) scale (Crandall *et al.*, 1965) and the
Health Locus of Control (HLC) scale (Wallston *et al.*, 1978; Wallston *et al.*, 1976). Although dealing with more circumscribed behavioral domains than the original I–E scale, these measures are still
quite general and they thus fail to be strictly compatible with any
particular action. As might therefore be expected, the prediction of
specific behavior from the IAR and HLC scales has also met with
only very qualified success [see Lefcourt (1982) and Wallston and
Wallston (1981) for relevant literature reviews]. In the domain of
achievement-related behavior, results tend to confirm a positive, if
often weak, relation between internality and performance (see
Bar-Tal and Bar-Zohar, 1977); however, the data also contain
"paradoxical inconsistencies or failures at replication" (Lefcourt,
1982, p. 98). A pattern of weak and inconsistent results is also found
in research that has used the HLC scale to predict such health-related
behaviors as seeking information about illness, preventive health
activities, smoking cessation, weight reduction, dental hygiene, and
adherence to medical regimens. In their review of this research area,
Wallston and Wallston (1981, p. 236) reached the following rather
pessimistic conclusion:

> Human behavior is complex and multidetermined. It is simplis-
> tic to believe that health locus of control beliefs will ever predict
> very much of the variance in health behavior by itself [*sic*].

However, in terms of conceptualizing control beliefs that are
compatible with a particular behavior of interest, one need not stop
at the level of perceived achievement responsibility or health locus of
control. Instead, one can consider perceived control over a given
behavior or behavioral goal. Along those lines, Bandura (1977,
1982) has introduced the concept of perceived *self-efficacy* which
refers to the subjective probability that one is capable of executing a
certain course of action. Bandura *et al.* (1977) showed that such
self-efficacy beliefs correlate strongly with coping behavior. Adult
snake phobics received one of two treatments: participant modeling
(going through a series of interactions with a snake, assisted by the
therapist) or modeling (observation) only. Immediately following
treatment, the participants rated the likelihood that they would be
capable of performing each of 18 tasks involving a snake (self-

efficacy beliefs). During the subsequent performance test, they were actually asked to perform the graded series of behaviors which ranged from looking at, touching, and holding the snake to letting the snake loose in the room and retrieving it. The correlations between perceived self-efficacy and performance were 0.83 and 0.84 in the two treatment conditions, respectively.

The Locke *et al.* (1984) study mentioned earlier also revealed a strong relation between self-efficacy beliefs and behavioral achievement. Remember that the performance criterion in this study was the number of uses for common objects listed in a short period of time. Following a few practice trials, participants expressed their certainty, in percentage points, that they could list varying numbers of uses. These measures of perceived self-efficacy had a correlation of 0.54 with the actual number of uses listed.

Closely related to self-efficacy beliefs is Ajzen's (1985; Ajzen and Madden, 1986; Schifter and Ajzen, 1985) concept of *perceived behavioral control*. Consistent with the principle of compatibility, it has been shown (Ajzen and Timko, 1986) that perceived control over specific health-related behaviors is far superior to the more general health locus of control scale in predicting corresponding actions. College students reported the frequency with which they performed each of 24 health-related behaviors, such as staying out of smoke-filled rooms, taking vitamin supplements, performing cancer self-examinations, and getting periodic T. B. tests. The health locus of control was assessed by means of the Wallston *et al.* (1978) scale, while perceived control with respect to each behavior was indexed by asking respondents to rate, on a 7-point scale, how easy or difficult they considered performance of the behavior to be. Internal health locus of control correlated, on average, 0.10 with the 24 individual behaviors. In contrast, the average correlation between perceived behavioral control and performance of the corresponding behavior was 0.77.

Alagna and Reddy (1984) also reported fairly strong correlations between perceived control and behavioral performance in the health domain. Women completed a questionnaire which, among other things, assessed their beliefs that breast self-examinations can detect lesions, that they were familiar with correct self-examination techniques, and that they could detect lesions in their breasts by means of self-examinations. These three items were summed to yield a measure of perceived control over performing correct breast self-examinations.[5] In addition, the women indicated how frequently they had performed breast self-examinations in the previous 6 months. Following administration of the questionnaire, the women were observed performing a breast examination on a synthetic model, and the proficiency of these examinations was scored by trained observers in terms of the number of correct behaviors performed. The correlation of perceived behavioral control with frequency of self-examinations was 0.45; with behavioral proficiency it was found to be 0.57.

The research described in this section suggests that specific dispositional measures can predict and to some extent account for corresponding behavioral tendencies. Of particular interest in this respect is the concept of perceived control. When reduced to the level of specific response tendencies, perceived self-efficacy or perceived control over performance of a behavior is found to correlate strongly with actual performance. By considering perceived behavioral control we begin to gain an understanding of the factors that influence the performance of specific actions. Of course, other factors are also involved and we will consider one other factor below. At this point we merely note that, as a general rule, people attempt to perform a behavior to the extent that they have confidence in their ability to do so. Their attempts are successful if they in fact are capable of performing the behavior in question. We will return to this issue in Chapter 6 where we will examine the concept of perceived behavioral control in greater detail.

## Attitudes and specific response tendencies

According to the principle of compatibility we should be able to predict individual behaviors (directed at a certain target) from measures of attitudes toward those behaviors. By and large, the literature lends support to this expectation. For example, Kothandapani (1971) assessed the attitudes of married women toward personal use of birth control methods by means of 12 standard scales. The self-reported use or nonuse of such methods served as the behavioral criterion. All 12 attitude–behavior correlations were found to be signi cant, with an average coefficient of 0.69. Similarly, Veevers (1971) used five different instruments to measure attitudes toward drinking alcoholic beverages. Self-reports of actual drinking among residents of two Alberta communities could be predicted from these attitudes with coefficients ranging from 0.46 to 0.72.

Manstead *et al.* (1983) reported a study on infant feeding practices. Toward the end of their pregnancies, women completed a questionnaire that assessed, among other things, their attitudes toward breast-feeding (as opposed to bottle-feeding) their babies. Six weeks following delivery, a questionnaire sent to each woman ascertained her actual feeding practices during the preceding 6 weeks. Attitudes toward the behavior of interest were found to have a correlation of 0.67 with the feeding method employed.

In two laboratory studies, Ajzen (1971; Ajzen and Fishbein, 1970) attempted to predict cooperative behavior in different "Prisoner's Dilemma" games. In these games, two players can each choose between two possible moves, and their joint choices determine how much each player wins or loses (their pay-offs). One option in the game represents a cooperative move, the other a competitive move. The participants in the studies were pairs of same-sex college students who played three Prisoner's Dilemma games that varied in their pay-off matrices. Following a few practice trials, the players were asked to complete a questionnaire that included two semantic differential measures of attitude, each comprised of four or five bipolar evaluative scales. These scales were used to obtain measures of attitude toward choosing the cooperative strategy and of attitude toward the other player. The proportion of cooperative strategy choices following completion of the questionnaire served as the behavioral criterion. Looking at the three games played in the two experiments, the actual choice of cooperative moves correlated 0.63, 0.70 and 0.65 with attitude toward choosing the cooperative strategy. By way of comparison, the correlations between attitude toward the other player (a global attitude) and cooperative game behavior were very low and not always significant ($r = 0.26$, 0.09 and 0.27, respectively).

As a final example, consider a study conducted during the 1974 general election in Great Britain (Fishbein *et al.*, 1976). Voters were interviewed prior to the election and their attitudes toward voting for each candidate in their constituencies were assessed by means of an evaluative semantic differential. The average correlation between these attitude measures and actual voting choice was 0.85. More general attitudes toward the candidates themselves also predicted voting behavior, but here the average correlation was only 0.51, significantly lower than the correlation obtained by measuring attitudes toward the act of voting for or against the competing candidates.

To summarize briefly, in this section we have identified a second determinant of specific response tendencies, namely, attitude toward the behavior in question. Like perceptions of behavioral control, attitudes toward a behavior are found to correlate well with the corresponding behavior, and since they can be assessed ahead of time they can be used to predict behavioral performance. Beyond permitting prediction, however, the attitude toward the behavior concept can also enhance our understanding of the reasons why people exhibit or fail to exhibit a certain behavioral tendency. The studies reviewed above have shown that, as a general rule, people are likely to perform a specific behavior if they view its performance favorably, and they are unlikely to perform it if they view its performance unfavorably. Of course, this is only a first step toward an explanation. We need to know much more about the ways in which favorable or unfavorable attitudes toward behaviors are formed before we can feel confident that we have a good understanding of the factors involved. Chapter 6 deals with these factors in some detail.

## Summary and conclusions

The principle of compatibility points the way toward dispositional prediction of specific behavioral tendencies. With varying implications, attitudes and personality traits can be reduced to the level of a particular behavior, and such behavior-specific dispositions are found to correlate well with compatible action tendencies. In the case of traits, reduction to the level of individual response tendencies often involves the prediction of behavior from prior behavior or from self-reports of behavior and it is accomplished at considerable expense. Prior behavior becomes a poor predictor of later behavior as soon as circumstances change sufficiently to require modification of the behavior; and self-reports can be biased when we are dealing with highly sensitive issues. Moreover, even when consistency of a given behavioral tendency with prior behavior or with behavioral self-reports is observed, such consistency demonstrates merely that the same specific disposition can be assessed in different ways and at different points in time. It tells us little about the nature of the disposition and it does not add much to our understanding of the underlying causes of the behavior. In fact, it is generally true that personality traits, in and of themselves, have only limited explanatory power. It is not particularly illuminating to say that a person appears on time for appointments because she has a tendency to be punctual, or that she smiles easily because she is friendly. The personality trait itself is inferred from behavior, observed or reported; what explanatory value it does have lies in the fact that it accounts for a specific behavioral tendency (e.g. showing up on time for appointments) in terms of a more general response disposition (e.g. punctuality). However, when – in line with the principle of compatibility – the "trait" used to predict a behavior is the tendency to perform that very behavior, its explanatory power is lost entirely. One behavior-specific personality trait that can to a large extent escape these limitations is the belief in self-efficacy or control over a given behavior. Perceived behavioral control is found to correlate well with the tendency to perform the behavior and it provides at least a partial explanation for the tendency in question.

A reduction of attitudes to the level of individual behaviors is accomplished without much difficulty. The same methods that are used to assess attitudes toward objects, institutions, or events can be applied directly to the construction of scales that assess attitudes toward a given behavior. Such behavior-specific attitudes correlate well with the corresponding behavior and, like perceived behavioral control, they can help explain why people act the way they do.

## Notes

1. Although self-reports are generally considered inferior to direct observations of behavior, they often have the advantage of reflecting a summary judgment based on performance or nonperformance of the behavior on a variety of occasions; that is, self-reports of behavior can be viewed as intuitive estimates of behavioral tendencies across occasions (see also Epstein, 1983b).
2. I am grateful to Amiram Vinokur for providing a summary of these data.
3. These correlations contrast with correlations of 0.58, 0.55 and 0.38 for behavioral aggregates computed in accordance with the principle of aggregation.
4. Even when biased, self-reports can correlate well with actual behavior. For instance, if all respondents tend to under-report the number of cigarettes they smoke by about the same amount, the reported number smoked will be lower than the actual number, but the correlation between the two may still be high.
5. The first of these three items is conceptually different from perceived

behavioral control, and it indeed had a lower correlation with effective breast self-examination than did the other two items. However, all three items correlated highly with each other, a finding which prompted the investigators to combine them into a single measure.

## Suggestions for further readings

1. Ajzen, I. (1982). On behaving in accordance with one's attitudes. In M. P. Zanna, E. T. Higgins and C. P. Herman (Eds), *Consistency in social behavior: The Ontario Symposium*, Vol. 2, pp. 3–15. Hillsdale, NJ: Lawrence Erlbaum Associates. This chapter provides an easy introduction to the principle of compatibility, in the context of the attitude–behavior relation.
2. Bandura, A. (1982). Self-efficacy mechanism in human agency. *American Psychologist*, 37, 122–47. In this article, Bandura discusses his theory of self-efficacy, and presents the results of some empirical research on the self-efficacy concept.

# 6 / FROM INTENTIONS TO ACTIONS

It's a long step from saying to doing.

*Cervantes*

In the previous chapter we began to unravel the mystery surrounding prediction and explanation of specific action tendencies by turning our attention to behavioral dispositions that correspond precisely to the particular action tendency of interest. Based on this principle of compatibility, the present chapter introduces a conceptual framework for the prediction of specific action tendencies, a framework that deals with a limited set of dispositional antecedents assumed to guide specific action tendencies, with the origins of these dispositions, and with the relations among them. Incorporated into this conceptual framework are the two behavior-specific dispositions discussed in Chapter 5 – perceived behavioral control and attitude toward the behavior – as well as a few additional concepts required for a more complete account of the determinants of specific action tendencies.

## The case of willful behavior

Many behaviors in everyday life, which are often the behaviors of greatest interest to personality and social psychologists, can be thought of as being largely under volitional control. That is to say, people can easily perform these behaviors if they are so inclined, or refrain from performing them if they decide against it. In Western countries most people can, if they so desire, vote in political elections, watch the evening news on television, buy toothpaste at a drugstore, pray at a nearby church or synagogue, or donate blood to their local hospitals. If they wish, they may also decide against engaging in any of these activities.

The important point about willful behaviors of this kind is that their occurrence is a direct result of deliberate attempts made by an individual. The process involved can be described as follows. In accordance with deliberations to be described below, a person forms an *intention* to engage in a certain behavior. Intentions are assumed to capture the motivational factors that have an impact on a behavior; they are indications of how hard people are willing to try, of how much of an effort they are planning to exert, in order to perform the behavior. These intentions remain behavioral dispositions until, at the appropriate time and opportunity, an attempt is made to translate the intention into action. Assuming that the behavior is in fact under volitional control, the attempt will produce the desired act. This implies that the disposition most closely linked to a specific action tendency is the intention to perform the action under consideration. In other words, when dealing with volitional behavior people can be expected to do what they intend to do. Expressions of behavioral intention should thus permit a highly accurate prediction of corresponding volitional action.

## Predicting behavior from intention

The literature contains many examples of intentions that are highly correlated with volitional behavior. Table 6.1 shows a few representative findings. It can be seen that intentions have been found to predict a variety of corresponding action tendencies, ranging from simple strategy choices in laboratory games to actions of appreciable personal or social significance, such as having an abortion, smoking marijuana, and choosing among candidates in an election. It is worth noting that the intentions assessed in these studies were highly compatible with the behaviors in terms of the target, action, context, and time elements. Thus, in the study reported by King (1975), the behavior of interest was whether or not college students would attend church services in the course of a 2-week vacation. This behavior could be predicted with a high degree of accuracy by asking the students, prior to the recess, how likely it was that they would attend church services at least every 2 weeks.

Available evidence also supports the idea that intentions are close antecedents of overt actions. If intentions are indeed the immediate

*Table 6.1*    Correlations between intentions and volitional behaviors

| Behavior | Intention–behavior correlation |
|---|---|
| Cooperation in Prisoner's Dilemma game (Ajzen, 1971) | 0.82 |
| Having an abortion (Smetana and Adler, 1980) | 0.96 |
| Using birth control pills (see Ajzen and Fishbein, 1980, Ch. 11) | 0.85 |
| Breast- *vs.* bottle-feeding (Manstead *et al.*, 1983) | 0.82 |
| Smoking marijuana (Ajzen *et al.*, 1982) | 0.72 |
| Attending church during the Easter holiday (King, 1975) | 0.90 |
| Voting choice in presidential election (see Ajzen and Fishbein, 1980, Ch. 13) | 0.80 |

*Note:* All correlations are significant ($P < 0.05$).

determinants of volitional behavior then they should correlate more strongly with the behavior than do other kinds of antecedent factors. Consistent with this argument, the predictive validity of intentions is typically found to be significantly greater than that of attitudes toward the behavior. Consider, for example, the study by Manstead *et al.* (1983) on the prediction of breast-feeding versus bottle-feeding of newborn infants. As we saw in Chapter 5, mothers' attitudes toward these alternative feeding practices had a correlation of 0.67 with the feeding method they actually employed. By way of comparison, inspection of Table 6.1 shows that the intention–behavior correlation in this study was 0.82. Very similar results were obtained with respect to cooperation in Prisoner's Dilemma games (Ajzen, 1971; Ajzen and Fishbein, 1970). In Chapter 5, the correlations between attitudes toward choosing the cooperative alternative and actual game behavior were reported to have ranged from 0.63 to 0.70. When predicted from intentions, correlations with game behavior were found to be in the 0.82–0.85 range.

Another example is contained in a study by Ajzen *et al.* (1982). The use of marijuana by college students served as one of the behavioral criteria in this study. The students evaluated "my smoking marijuana in the next 3 or 4 weeks" on a set of semantic

differential scales and also indicated, on a 7-point scale,
hood that they would perform this behavior. About 4 v
they were contacted by telephone and asked to indicate whether oi
not they had smoked marijuana during the time that had passed. In
Table 6.1 it can be seen that this self-report of marijuana use
correlated 0.72 with intentions; its correlation with attitude toward
smoking marijuana was, at 0.53, significantly lower.

## Stability of intentions

Intentions are thus closely linked to volitional actions and can
predict them with a high degree of accuracy. This is not to say,
however, that a measure of intention will always correlate strongly
with the corresponding behavior. Clearly, intentions can change
over time; the longer the time interval, the greater the likelihood that
unforeseen events will produce changes in intentions. A measure of
intention obtained before the changes took place cannot be expected
to predict behavior accurately. It follows that accuracy of prediction
will usually decline with the amount of time that intervenes between
measurement of intention and observation of behavior. Imagine, for
example, a woman who intends to vote for the Democratic candidate
in a race for the United States Senate. After her intention is assessed,
she learns – by watching a television interview with the candidate a
few days before the election – that he opposes abortion and equal
rights for women. As a result, she "changes her mind," decides to
vote for the Republican candidate instead, and actually does so in the
election. Her actual voting choice corresponds to her most recent
intention, but it could not have been predicted from the measure of
intention obtained at the earlier point in time.

Several studies have demonstrated the disruptive effects of unforeseen events. For instance, Songer-Nocks (1976a, 1976b) assessed
intentions to choose the cooperative alternative at the beginning of a
20-trial, two-person experimental game. One-half of the pairs of
players were given feedback after each trial which informed them
about the choices made by their partners and of the pay-offs to each
player. The other pairs were given no such information. Feedback
concerning the partner's competitive or cooperative behavior
may, of course, influence a player's own intentions regarding
future moves in the game. Consistent with this argument, Songer-
Nocks reported that providing feedback significantly reduced the
accuracy with which initial intentions predicted actual game
behavior.

More indirect evidence regarding the disruptive effects of unanticipated events is available from studies that have varied the amount of
time between the assessment of intentions and observation of behavior. Since the likelihood of unforeseen events will tend to increase
as time passes, we would expect to find stronger intention–behavior
correlations with short rather than long periods of delay. Fishbein
and Coombs (1974) reported findings in support of this expectation.
In this study, intentions to vote for Goldwater in the 1964 United
States presidential election correlated 0.80 with self-reported voting
choice when the intention was measured 1 month prior to the
election and 0.89 when it was measured during the week preceding
the election. Sejwacz *et al.* (1980) also obtained support for the
disruptive potential of temporal delay in a study of weight loss. A
sample of college women indicated their intentions to perform eight
weight-reducing behaviors (avoid snacking between meals, participate in sports on a regular basis, etc.) at the beginning of a 2-month
period and again 1 month later. Correlations were computed between initial intentions and reported behavior over the 2-month
period, and between subsequent intentions and reported behavior
during the final month. As expected, intention–behavior correlations were stronger for the 1-month period than for the 2-month
period. For example, the correlation between intention to avoid long
periods of inactivity and performance of this behavior (as recorded
by the women in weekly logs) was higher when the time period was 1
month ($r = 0.72$) than when it was 2 months ($r = 0.47$). Considering
all eight behaviors, the average correlation increased from 0.51 for
the 2-month period to 0.67 for the 1-month period.

*Explaining volitional behavior: a theory of reasoned action*

The finding that intentions often predict behavior quite accurately
does not in itself provide much information about the reasons for the
behavior. Beyond confirming that the behavior in question is under
volitional control, it is not very illuminating to discover that people
do what they intend to do. Since we are interested in *understanding*
human behavior, not merely in predicting it, we must try to identify
the determinants of behavioral intentions. Ajzen and Fishbein's
(1980; Fishbein and Ajzen, 1975) theory of reasoned action, mentioned in Chapter 2, is designed to accomplish precisely this goal;

that is, the theory is concerned with the causal antecedents of volitional behavior.

As its name implies, the theory of reasoned action is based on the assumption that human beings usually behave in a sensible manner; that they take account of available information and implicitly or explicitly consider the implications of their actions. Consistent with its focus on volitional behavior, and in line with the findings reported earlier, the theory postulates that a person's intention to perform (or not to perform) a behavior is the immediate determinant of that action. Barring unforeseen events, people are expected to act in accordance with their intentions.

*Attitudes and subjective norms*

According to the theory of reasoned action, intentions are a function of two basic determinants, one personal in nature and the other reflecting social influence. The personal factor is the individual's *attitude toward the behavior*, first encountered in Chapter 5 and again earlier in this chapter. Unlike general attitudes toward institutions, people, or objects that have traditionally been studied by social psychologists, this attitude is the individual's positive or negative evaluation of performing the particular behavior of interest. The second determinant of intention is the person's perception of social pressure to perform or not to perform the behavior under consideration. Since it deals with perceived normative prescriptions, this factor is termed *subjective norm*. Generally speaking, people intend to perform a behavior when they evaluate it positively and when they believe that important others think they should perform it.

The theory assumes that the relative importance of attitude toward the behavior and subjective norm depends in part on the intention under investigation. For some intentions attitudinal considerations are more important than normative considerations, while for other intentions normative considerations predominate. Frequently, both factors are important determinants of the intention. In addition, the relative weights of the attitudinal and normative factors may vary from one person to another. Figure 6.1 is a graphic representation of the theory of reasoned action as described up to this point.

Many studies have provided strong support for the hypothesized links between intention as the dependent variable and attitude toward the behavior and subjective norm as the independent variables. Most studies have used multiple linear regression procedures

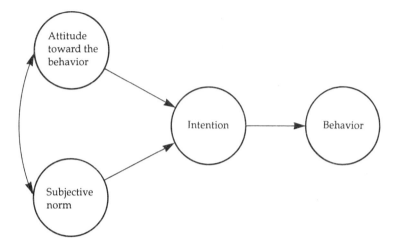

*Figure 6.1*   Theory of reasoned action

to estimate, in terms of a multiple correlation $(R)$, the simultaneous predictive power of attitudes and subjective norms, as well as the relative contributions of the two predictors in terms of standardized regression coefficients. Table 6.2 shows the results obtained in the studies discussed earlier (see Table 6.1) as well as a few additional examples. It can be seen that, with respect to a variety of different intentions, consideration of attitudes and subjective norms permitted highly accurate prediction. The multiple correlations in the studies listed ranged from 0.73 to 0.89. The relative importance of the two predictors is revealed by inspecting columns 3 and 4. In all cases, attitudes and subjective norms both made significant contributions to the prediction of intentions, although in eight of the ten studies, the relative contribution of attitudes exceeded that of subjective norms. Perhaps not surprisingly, however, women's decisions to have an abortion, and a couple's decision to have another child, were more strongly affected by perceived social pressure than by personal attitudes.

For many practical purposes this level of explanation may be sufficient. We can to some extent account for the intentions people form by examining their attitudes toward the behavior, their subjective norms, and the relative importance of these two factors. However, for a more complete understanding of intentions it is necessary to explore why people hold certain attitudes and subjective norms.

*Table* 6.2 Prediction of intentions from attitude toward the behavior ($A_B$) and subjective norm (*SN*)

| Intention | Correlation coefficients | | Regression coefficients | | Multiple correlation |
|---|---|---|---|---|---|
| | $A_B$ | *SN* | $A_B$ | *SN* | *R* |
| Cooperation in Prisoner's Dilemma game (Ajzen, 1971) | 0.75 | 0.69 | 0.53 | 0.40 | 0.82 |
| Having an abortion (Smetana and Adler, 1980) | 0.50 | 0.69 | 0.21 | 0.46 | 0.76 |
| Using birth control pills (see Ajzen and Fishbein, 1980, Ch. 11) | 0.81 | 0.68 | 0.64 | 0.41 | 0.89 |
| Breast- *vs.* bottle-feeding (Manstead *et al.*, 1983) | 0.73 | 0.60 | 0.61 | 0.22 | 0.78 |
| Smoking marijuana (Ajzen *et al.*, 1982) | 0.79 | 0.45 | 0.74 | 0.13 | 0.80 |
| Attending church (King, 1975) | 0.74 | 0.59 | 0.62 | 0.20 | 0.76 |
| Voting choice (see Ajzen and Fishbein, 1980, Ch. 13) | 0.81 | 0.71 | 0.61 | 0.27 | 0.79 |
| Having another child (Vinokur-Kaplan, 1978) | 0.65 | 0.83 | 0.19 | 0.70 | 0.85 |
| Buying Miller beer (see Ajzen and Fishbein, 1980, Ch. 12) | 0.76 | 0.63 | 0.60 | 0.27 | 0.79 |
| Joining an alcoholic treatment unit (see Ajzen and Fishbein, 1980, Ch. 15) | 0.69 | 0.67 | 0.43 | 0.37 | 0.73 |

*Note:* All coefficients are statistically significant ($P < 0.05$).

**Antecedents of attitudes toward a behavior**    In Chapter 2 we discussed, in general terms, the formation of attitudes within the framework of the theory of reasoned action. There we showed how evaluations of any object follow reasonably from the beliefs we hold about the object. We can now apply these ideas to the formation of attitudes toward a behavior. According to the theory of reasoned action, attitude toward a behavior is determined by salient beliefs about that behavior, termed *behavioral beliefs*. Each behavioral belief links the behavior to a certain outcome, or to some other attribute such as the cost incurred by performing the behavior. For example, a person may believe that "going on a low sodium diet" (the behavior) "reduces blood pressure," "leads to a change in life style," "severely restricts the range of approved foods," and so forth (outcomes). The attitude toward the behavior is determined by the person's evaluation of the outcomes associated with the behavior and by the strength of these associations. As we see in Chapter 2, the evaluation of each salient outcome contributes to the attitude in proportion to the person's subjective probability that the behavior will produce the outcome in question. By multiplying belief strength and outcome evaluation, and summing the resulting products, we obtain an estimate of the attitude toward the behavior, an estimate based on the person's salient beliefs about the behavior. This expectancy-value model is described symbolically in Equation 6.1, where $A_B$ stands for attitude toward behavior $B$; $b_i$ is the belief (subjective probability) that performing behavior $B$ will lead to outcome $i$; $e_i$ is the evaluation of outcome $i$; and the sum is over the $n$ salient beliefs. It can be seen that, generally speaking, a person who believes that performing a given behavior will lead to mostly positive outcomes will hold a favorable attitude toward performing the behavior, whereas a person who believes that performing the behavior will lead to mostly negative outcomes will hold an unfavorable attitude.

$$A_B \propto \sum_n b_i e_i \qquad (6.1)$$

Several of the studies cited earlier have reported data that confirm the expectancy-value model of attitude described in Equation 6.1. For example, King (1975) assessed behavioral beliefs concerning the advantages and disadvantages of attending church services at least every 2 weeks as well as evaluations of these outcomes. Responses were used to compute an estimate of attitude toward attending church services in accordance with Equation 6.1. In addition, King used an evaluative semantic differential to obtain a relatively direct measure of the same attitude. The correlation between the direct evaluation of the behavior and the belief-based measure was found to be 0.69. High correlations between direct and belief-based measures of attitude have also been reported with respect to such behaviors as voting choice in a United States presidential election ($r = 0.79$), using birth control pills ($r = 0.79$), and choice of a career orientation ($r = 0.81$) (see Ajzen and Fishbein, 1980).

**Antecedents of subjective norms**  Subjective norms, the second major determinant of intentions in the theory of reasoned action, are also assumed to be a function of beliefs, but beliefs of a different kind, namely the person's beliefs that specific individuals or groups approve or disapprove of performing the behavior. Serving as a point of reference to guide behavior, these individuals and groups are known as *referents*. For many behaviors, the important referents include a person's parents, spouse, close friends, coworkers, and, depending on the behavior involved, perhaps such experts as physicians or tax accountants. The beliefs that underlie subjective norms are termed *normative beliefs*. Generally speaking, people who believe that most referents with whom they are motivated to comply think they should perform the behavior will perceive social pressure to do so. Conversely, people who believe that most referents with whom they are motivated to comply would disapprove of their performing the behavior will have a subjective norm that puts pressure on them to avoid performing the behavior. The relation between normative beliefs and subjective norm is expressed symbolically in Equation 6.2. Here, $SN$ is the subjective norm; $b_j$ is the normative belief concerning referent $j$; $m_j$ is the person's motivation to comply with referent $j$; and $n$ is the number of salient normative beliefs.

$$SN \propto \sum_n b_j m_j \qquad (6.2)$$

Subjective norms can be assessed in a relatively direct manner by asking respondents to judge how likely it is that most people who are important to them would approve of their performing a given behavior. Such direct measures have been compared with belief-based estimates of subjective norms, computed in accordance with Equation 6.2. Correlations between the two types of measures are generally quite high, ranging from 0.60 to 0.80 (see Ajzen and Fishbein, 1980).

The discussion up to this point shows how volitional behavior can be explained in terms of a limited number of concepts. Through a series of intervening steps the theory of reasoned action traces the causes of behavior to the person's salient beliefs. Each successive step in this sequence from behavior to beliefs provides a more comprehensive account of the factors that determine the behavior. At the initial level behavior is assumed to be determined by intention. At the next level these intentions are themselves explained in terms of attitudes toward the behavior and subjective norms. The third level accounts for attitudes and subjective norms in terms of beliefs about the consequences of performing the behavior and about the normative expectations of relevant referents. In the final analysis, then, a person's behavior is explained by considering his or her beliefs. Since people's beliefs represent the information (be it correct or incorrect) they have about themselves and about the world around them, it follows that their behavior is ultimately determined by this information.[1]

### The informational foundation of behavior

A concrete example may help clarify the role of beliefs in determining the performance of a specific behavior. Manstead *et al.* (1983) compared the beliefs of mothers who breast-fed their babies with mothers who used the bottle-feeding method. Based on prior research in the field, the investigators selected the six reasons women cite most frequently for breast-feeding their babies and the six reasons they cite most frequently for bottle-feeding their babies. With respect to each of these 12 salient behavioral beliefs, women about to give birth were asked to provide two measures: their subjective probabilities that a given feeding method is associated with the cited consequence, and their evaluations of that consequence. The following are examples for each feeding method.

*Behavioral beliefs*

Breast-feeding protects a baby against infection

likely :__:__:__:__:__:__:__: unlikely

Bottle-feeding provides incomplete nourishment for a baby

likely :__:__:__:__:__:__:__: unlikely

*Outcome evaluations*

Using a feeding method that protects a baby against infection is

very important :__:__:__:__:__:__: completely un-
to me                                          important to me

Using a feeding method that provides complete nourishment
for my baby is

very important :__:__:__:__:__:__: completely un-
to me                                          important to me

Table 6.3 shows the average likelihood rating (7 = likely, 1 =
unlikely) provided by mothers who breast-fed their babies and
mothers who bottle-fed their babies. Statistical significance between
the two groups is indicated. As can be seen, the two groups of
mothers differed significantly on all six of the behavioral beliefs
about breast feeding. Examination of these differences reveals some
of the reasons for choosing one or the other feeding method.
Although all women tended to agree that breast-feeding establishes a
close bond between mother and baby, the women who held this

*Table 6.3*  Mean behavioral belief ratings (after Manstead *et al.*, 1983)

| Behavioral beliefs | Mothers who breast-fed | Mothers who bottle-fed |
|---|---|---|
| *About breast feeding* | | |
| Establishes close bond between mother and baby | 6.61 | 5.45[a] |
| Is embarrassing for mother | 4.93 | 4.00[a] |
| Is good for mother's figure | 5.98 | 4.45[a] |
| Limits mother's social life | 3.90 | 3.13[a] |
| Provides best nourishment for baby | 6.77 | 5.57[a] |
| Protects baby against infection | 6.48 | 5.39[a] |
| *About bottle feeding* | | |
| Is a very convenient method of feeding baby | 4.47 | 6.16[a] |
| Provides incomplete nourishment for baby | 4.52 | 4.91 |
| Makes it possible for baby's father to be involved in feeding | 5.56 | 6.35[a] |
| Is an expensive feeding method | 2.66 | 2.80 |
| Is a trouble-free feeding method | 3.29 | 4.80[a] |
| Allows one to see exactly how much milk baby has had | 6.13 | 6.25 |

[a] Significant difference between breast- and bottle-feeding mothers ($P < 0.05$).

*Table 6.4*   Mean outcome evaluations (after Manstead *et al.*, 1983)

| Outcomes | Mothers who breast-fed | Mothers who bottle-fed |
| --- | --- | --- |
| Allows me to go out socially | 2.94 | 3.45 |
| Is good for my figure | 5.02 | 4.07[a] |
| Is convenient | 4.69 | 5.22 |
| Establishes a close bond between me and my baby | 6.75 | 6.13[a] |
| Does not make me feel embarrassed | 3.80 | 4.81[a] |
| Allows baby's father to be involved in feeding | 4.32 | 6.15[a] |
| Provides complete nourishment for baby | 6.94 | 6.72[a] |
| Is trouble-free | 4.39 | 4.24 |
| Is inexpensive | 4.02 | 3.55 |
| Allows one to see exactly how much milk baby has had | 4.09 | 6.06[a] |
| Protects my baby against infection | 6.86 | 6.56[a] |

[a] Significant difference between breast- and bottle-feeding mothers ($P < 0.05$).

belief more strongly were more likely to choose the breast-feeding method. In a similar vein, the choice of breast-feeding increased with the perceived likelihood that this method is good for the mother's figure, provides the best nourishment for a baby, and protects a baby against infection. On the other hand, the more a woman believed that breast-feeding is embarrassing for the mother or limits her social life, the less likely she was to use this method.

With respect to the bottle-feeding method, the two groups of mothers differed significantly on only three of the six behavioral beliefs. An examination of the significant differences shows that perceived outcomes of bottle-feeding which best explained the choice of this method were the beliefs that it is a very convenient method, that it enables the father to be involved in feeding, and that it is a trouble-free feeding method.

It is possible, in a similar fashion, to compare the outcome evaluations of mothers who breast-fed their babies with those of mothers who chose the bottle-feeding method. Such a comparison provides additional information about the reasons for choosing one method over the other. Table 6.4 presents the average outcome evaluations for the two groups ($1$ = completely unimportant, $7$ = very important). Examining the six evaluations that distinguished significantly between the two groups, it can be seen that mothers tended to choose the breast-feeding method if, in comparison to mothers who chose the bottle-feeding method, they judged as relatively important the following outcomes: having a good figure, establishing a close bond with their babies, providing complete nourishment for their babies, and protecting their babies against infection. In addition, these mothers also rated as relatively unimportant the outcomes of feeling embarrassed, allowing the baby's father to be involved in the feeding, and being able to see exactly how much milk baby has had.

The study by Manstead *et al.* (1983) also reported interesting data concerning the effects of normative beliefs on the choice of breast-versus bottle-feeding. The salient normative referents identified in this context were the baby's father, the mother's own mother, her closest female friend, and her medical adviser (usually a gynecologist). With respect to each referent, normative beliefs about breast-feeding and about bottle-feeding were assessed, as was motivation to comply with each referent. The following scales illustrate the procedures used.

*Normative beliefs*

The baby's father thinks that I

definitely should :__:__:__:__:__:__:__: definitely should
breast-feed                                        not breast-feed

*Motivation to comply*

In general, how much do you care what the baby's father thinks you should do?

Do not care at all :__:__:__:__:__:__:__: Care very much

Table 6.5 shows the average normative beliefs for the two groups of mothers. The differences between mothers who breast-fed their babies and mothers who used the bottle are statistically significant for each normative belief. Inspection of the normative beliefs for mothers who used the breast-feeding method reveals that, in their opinions, important referents strongly preferred this method over the alternative bottle-feeding method. In contrast, women who believed that their referents had no strong preferences for either method were more likely to feed their babies by means of a bottle.

Finally, the mothers' average motivations to comply with each of the four salient referent individuals are presented in Table 6.6. Both groups of mothers were highly motivated to comply with the baby's

*Table 6.5*   Mean normative beliefs (after Manstead *et al.*, 1983)

| Normative beliefs | Mothers who breast-fed | Mothers who bottle-fed |
|---|---|---|
| *About breast feeding* | | |
| Baby's father | 6.21 | 4.45 |
| Own mother | 5.57 | 4.45 |
| Closest female friend | 5.39 | 4.47 |
| Medical adviser | 6.20 | 5.25 |
| *About bottle feeding* | | |
| Baby's father | 2.89 | 4.16 |
| Own mother | 3.24 | 3.99 |
| Closest female friend | 3.43 | 3.98 |
| Medical adviser | 2.96 | 3.55 |

*Note:* All differences between breast-feeding and bottle-feeding mothers are statistically significant ($P < 0.05$).

father, and they had moderately strong motivations to comply with their own mothers and closest female friends. The only significant difference emerged with respect to the women's medical advisers. Mothers who eventually decided to breast-feed their babies were more highly motivated to comply with their medical advisers than were mothers who eventually decided to use the bottle. This is consistent with the finding that the former mothers perceived their medical advisers to be strong advocates of the breast-feeding method (see Table 6.5).

To summarize briefly, research on the theory of reasoned action describes how people tend to proceed on a course of action in quite a deliberate manner. The initial considerations deal with the likely

*Table 6.6*   Mean motivations to comply (after Manstead *et al.*, 1983)

| Referent | Mothers who breast-fed | Mothers who bottle-fed |
|---|---|---|
| Baby's father | 6.07 | 5.61 |
| Own mother | 4.84 | 4.60 |
| Closest female friend | 3.38 | 3.52 |
| Medical adviser | 5.36 | 4.52[a] |

[a] Significant difference between breast- and bottle-feeding mothers ($P < 0.05$).

consequences of performing a certain behavior and expectations of important referent individuals or groups. Depending on the evaluation of the behavior's likely consequences and motivation to comply with referent sources, attitudes and subjective norms emerge that guide the formation of behavioral intentions. Barring unforeseen events that might change the intentions, and contingent on the behavior being under volitional control, the intentions are carried out under appropriate circumstances.

## The case of incomplete volitional control

The theory of reasoned action was developed explicitly to deal with purely volitional behaviors. In this context it has proved quite successful. Complications are encountered, however, when we try to apply the theory to behaviors that are not fully under volitional control. A well-known example is that many smokers intend to quit but, when they try, fail to attain their goal. In the theory of reasoned action, intentions are the prime motivating force and they mediate the effects of other factors, i.e. of attitude toward the behavior and of subjective norm. The stronger are people's intentions to engage in a behavior or to achieve their behavioral goals, the more successful they are expected to be. However, the degree of success will depend not only on one's desire or intention, but also on such partly nonmotivational factors as availability of requisite opportunities and resources. To the extent that people have the required opportunities and resources, and intend to perform the behavior, they should succeed in doing so.

At first glance, the problem of behavioral control may appear to apply to a limited range of actions only. Closer scrutiny reveals, however, that even very mundane activities, which can usually be executed (or not executed) at will, are sometimes subject to the influence of factors beyond one's control. Such a simple behavior as driving to the supermarket may be thwarted by mechanical trouble with the car. Control over behavior can thus best be viewed as a continuum. On one extreme are behaviors that encounter few if any problems of control. A good case in point is voting choice: once the voter has entered the voting booth, selection among the candidates can be done at will. At the other extreme are events, such as sneezing or lowering one's blood pressure, over which we have very little or no control. Most behaviors, of course, fall somewhere in between these

extremes. People usually encounter few problems of control when trying to attend lectures or read a book, but problems of control are more readily apparent when they try to overcome such powerful habits as smoking or drinking or when they set their sights on such difficult-to-attain goals as becoming a movie star. Viewed in this light it becomes clear that, strictly speaking, most intended behaviors are best considered *goals* whose attainment is subject to some degree of uncertainty. We can thus speak of behavior-goal units, and of intentions as plans of action in pursuit of behavioral goals (Ajzen, 1985).

## Control factors

Many investigators have in recent years turned their attention to the question of volitional control (e.g. Kuhl, 1985; Liska, 1984; Sarver, 1983; Triandis, 1977). On the following pages we review some of the factors that can influence the degree of control a person has over a given behavior.

### Internal factors

Various factors internal to an individual can influence successful performance of an intended action. Some of these factors are readily modified by training and experience while others are more resistant to change.

**Information, skills, and abilities**    A person who intends to perform a behavior may, upon trying to do so, discover that he or she lacks the needed information, skills, or abilities. Everyday life is replete with examples. We may intend to convert another person to our own political views, to help a boy with his mathematics, or to repair a malfunctioning record player, but fail in our attempts because we lack the required verbal and social skills, knowledge of mathematics, or mechanical aptitudes. To be sure, with experience we tend to acquire some appreciation of our abilities; yet new situations arise frequently, and failure to achieve our goals due to the lack of requisite skills is the order of the day.

The lack of ability in an unusual sense is illustrated in a study by Vinokur-Kaplan (1978) who assessed a couple's intention to have another child the following year. When interviewed 12 months later, actually having given birth to a child correlated 0.55 with intentions, a correlation which, although significant, is lower than the intention–behavior correlation observed in many other contexts. Having another child is, of course, only partially under volitional control, since fecundity, miscarriage, and other factors also mediate attainment of this goal.

Finally, forgetting is an interesting type of internal factor frequently cited as a reason for failure to carry out an intention (see Kuhl, 1985). A planned appointment or a deadline intended to be met can "slip a person's mind". In their study on blood donation, Pomazal and Jaccard (1976) interviewed people who had indicated an intention to donate but whose names did not appear on the official donor list. Among the reasons frequently mentioned was that they had simply forgotten all about it.

**Emotions and compulsions** Skills, abilities, and information may present problems of behavioral control, but it is usually assumed that, at least in principle, these problems can be overcome. In contrast, some types of behavior are subject to forces that seem to be largely beyond our control. People sometimes appear unable to cease thinking or dreaming about certain events, to stop stuttering, or to hold a tic in check. These compulsive behaviors are performed despite intentions and concerted efforts to the contrary.

Emotional behaviors seem to share some of the same characteristics. Individuals are often not held responsible for behaviors performed under stress or in the presence of strong emotions. We usually attribute little behavioral control to a person who is "overcome by emotion." Violent acts and poor performance are expected under such conditions, and there seems to be little we can do about it.

In sum, as we move beyond purely volitional acts, various internal factors may influence the successful performance of intended behavior. It may be fairly easy to gain control over some of these factors, as when we acquire the information or skills needed to perform a behavior. Other factors, such as intense emotions, stress or compulsions, are more difficult to neutralize.

*External factors*
Also impinging on a person's control over attainment of behavioral goals are situational or environmental factors external to the individual. These factors determine the extent to which circumstances facilitate or interfere with the performance of the behavior.

**Opportunity**    It takes little imagination to appreciate the importance of incidental factors or opportunities for the successful execution of an intended action. An intention to see a play cannot be
carried through if tickets are sold out on a particular night or if the
person is involved in a serious accident on the way to the theater. The
Pomazal and Jaccard (1976) study of blood donation again provides
relevant examples. When students who had failed to carry out their
intentions to donate blood were interviewed, they often mentioned
that such unforeseen obligations or events as exams, job interviews,
and coming down with a cold had prevented them from participating
in the blood drive. Given the presence of many disruptive factors, it is
hardly surprising that the correlation between intention and behavior was found to be of only moderate magnitude ($r = 0.52$). In
some instances, students came to give blood but were turned away
because of overcrowding. When these individuals were considered to
have performed the behavior, the intention–behavior correlation
increased to 0.59.

At first glance, lack of opportunity may appear equivalent to
occurrence of unanticipated events that bring about changes in
intentions, as discussed previously. While it is true that in the absence
of appropriate opportunities people may come to change their
intentions, there is an important difference between the two cases.
When new information becomes available after intentions have been
stated, the new information may affect salient beliefs about the
behavior and thus lead to changes in attitudes, subjective norms, and
intentions; at the end of this process the person is no longer interested
in carrying out the original intention. By way of contrast, lack of
opportunity disrupts an attempted behavior. Here, the person tries
to carry out the intention but fails because circumstances prevent
performance of the behavior. Although the immediate intention will
be affected, the basic underlying determinants need not have
changed.

Consider again the intention to see a particular play. Reading a
negative review or being told by a friend that the play is not worth
seeing may influence the person's beliefs such as to produce a more
negative attitude toward the intended behavior and perhaps also a
more negative subjective norm. As a result the person may no longer
intend to see the play on the night in question or on any other night,
unless and until other events again cause a change of mind. Contrast
this with the person who intends to see the play, drives to the theater,
but is told that there are no more tickets available. The environ-

mental obstacle to performance of the behavior will force a change of plan; but it need not change the person's attitude or subjective norm with respect to seeing the play. Instead, it may merely cause the person to try again on a different night.

Note also that lack of opportunity poses a problem only when the performance of a behavior on a single occasion is to be predicted. Behavioral tendencies across occasions are relatively unaffected because appropriate opportunities are likely to be present on at least some occasions.

**Dependence on others**  Whenever the performance of a behavior depends on the actions of other people, there exists the potential for incomplete control over behavioral goals. A good example of behavioral interdependence is the case of cooperation. One can cooperate with another person only if that person is also willing to cooperate. Experimental studies of cooperation and competition in laboratory games have provided ample evidence for this interdependence. For example, Ajzen and Fishbein (1970) reported correlations of 0.92 and 0.89 between cooperative strategy choices of the players in two Prisoner's Dilemma games. These high correlations suggest that a person's tendency to make cooperative choices depends on reciprocation by the other player.

As is true of time and opportunity, the inability to behave in accordance with intention because of dependence on others need not affect the underlying motivation. Often an individual who encounters difficulties related to interpersonal dependence may be able to perform the desired behavior in cooperation with a different partner. Sometimes, however, this may not be a viable course of action. A wife's adamant refusal to have more children will usually cause the husband eventually to abandon his plan to enlarge the family, rather than shift his effort to a different partner.

In short, lack of opportunity and dependence on others often lead only to temporary changes in intentions. When circumstances prevent the performance of a behavior, the person may wait for a better opportunity and, when another person fails to cooperate, a more compliant partner may be sought. However, when repeated efforts to perform the behavior result in failure, more fundamental changes in intentions can be expected.

*A theory of planned behavior*

The above discussion makes clear that many factors can disrupt the intention–behavior relation. Although volitional control is more likely to present a problem for some behaviors than for others, personal deficiencies and external obstacles can interfere with the performance of any behavior. Collectively, these factors represent people's *actual* control or lack of control over the behavior. [See also the discussions of "facilitating factors" by Triandis (1977), "the context of opportunity" by Sarver (1983), "resources" by Liska (1984) and "action control" by Kuhl (1985).] Given the problem's ubiquity, a behavioral intention can best be interpreted as an intention to *try* performing a certain behavior. A father's plan to take his children fishing next weekend is best viewed as an intention to try to make time for this activity, to prepare the required equipment, secure a fishing license, and so forth. The successful performance of the intended behavior is contingent on the person's control over the many factors that may prevent it. Of course, the conscious realization that we can only try to perform a given behavior will arise primarily when questions of control over the behavior are salient. Thus, people say that they will try to quit smoking or lose weight, but that they intend to go to church on Sunday. Nevertheless, even the intention to attend Sunday worship services must be viewed as an intention to try performing this behavior since factors beyond the individual's control can prevent its successful execution.

A recent attempt to provide a conceptual framework that addresses the problem of incomplete volitional control is Ajzen's *theory of planned behavior* (Ajzen, 1985; Ajzen and Madden, 1986; Schifter and Ajzen, 1985). This conceptual framework is an extension of the theory of reasoned action. As in the original model, a central factor in the theory of planned behavior is an individual's intention to perform the behavior of interest. In contrast to the original version, however, the theory of planned behavior postulates three, rather than two, conceptually independent determinants of intentions. The first two – attitude toward the behavior and subjective norm – are the same as before. The third and novel antecedent of intention is the degree of *perceived behavioral control*. This factor, discussed in Chapter 5, refers to the perceived ease or difficulty of performing the behavior and it is assumed to reflect past experience as well as anticipated impediments and obstacles. As a general rule, the more favorable the attitude and subjective norm

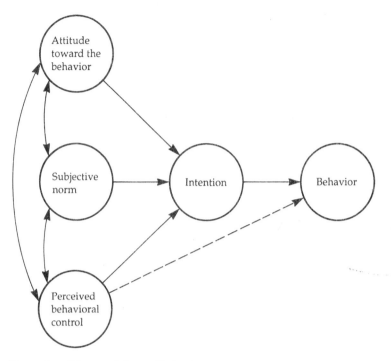

*Figure 6.2*    Theory of planned behavior

with respect to a behavior, and the greater the perceived behavioral control, the stronger should be the individual's intention to perform the behavior under consideration.

Note that the theory of planned behavior does not deal directly with the amount of control a person actually has in a given situation; instead, it considers the possible effects of *perceived* behavioral control on achievement of behavioral goals. Whereas intentions reflect primarily an individual's willingness to try enacting a given behavior, perceived control is likely to take into account some of the realistic constraints that may exist. To the extent that perceptions of behavioral control correspond reasonably well to actual control, they should provide useful information over and above expressed intentions. A structural model of the theory of planned behavior is shown in Figure 6.2.

Figure 6.2 shows two important features of the theory of planned behavior. First, the theory assumes that perceived behavioral control has motivational implications for intentions. People who believe that they have neither the resources nor the opportunities to perform a certain behavior are unlikely to form strong behavioral intentions to engage in it even if they hold favorable attitudes toward the behavior and believe that important others would approve of their performing the behavior. We thus expect an association between perceived behavioral control and intention that is not mediated by attitude and subjective norm. In Figure 6.2 this expectation is represented by the arrow linking perceived behavioral control to intention.

The second feature of interest is the possibility of a direct link between perceived behavioral control and behavior. As noted earlier, in many instances, the performance of a behavior depends not only on motivation to do so but also on adequate control over the behavior in question. It follows that perceived behavioral control can help predict goal attainment independent of behavioral intention to the extent that it reflects actual control with some degree of accuracy. In other words, perceived behavioral control can influence behavior indirectly, via intentions, and it can also be used to predict behavior directly because it may be considered a partial substitute for a measure of actual control.

Of course, in some situations perceived behavioral control is not particularly realistic. This is likely to be the case when the individual has little information about the behavior, when requirements or available resources have changed, or when new and unfamiliar elements have entered into the situation. Under those conditions a measure of perceived behavioral control may add little to the accuracy of behavioral prediction. The broken arrow in Figure 6.2 indicates that the link between perceived behavioral control and behavior is expected to emerge only when there is some agreement between perceptions of control and the person's actual control over the behavior.

Like the theory of reasoned action, the theory of planned behavior deals with the antecedents of attitudes, subjective norms and perceived behavioral control, antecedents which in the final analysis determine intentions and actions. Recall that, at the most basic level of explanation, behavior is assumed to be a function of salient information, or beliefs, relevant to the behavior. Three kinds of beliefs are distinguished: *behavioral beliefs* which are assumed to influence attitudes toward the behavior, *normative beliefs* which constitute the underlying determinants of subjective norms, and *control beliefs* which provide the basis for perceptions of behavioral control. Earlier we discussed the effects of behavioral beliefs on attitude toward the behavior, and the effects of normative beliefs on subjective norms. In a similar fashion, control beliefs are assumed to provide the basis for perceived behavioral control.

According to the theory of planned behavior, among the beliefs that ultimately determine intention and action is a set that deals with the presence or absence of requisite resources and opportunities. These beliefs may be based in part on past experience with the behavior, but they will usually also be influenced by second-hand information about the behavior, by observing the experiences of acquaintances and friends, and by other factors that increase or reduce the perceived difficulty of performing the behavior in question. The more resources and opportunities individuals think they possess, and the fewer obstacles or impediments they anticipate, the greater should be their perceived control over the behavior. As with behavioral and normative beliefs, it is possible to separate out these control beliefs and treat them as partially independent determinants of behavior. Just as beliefs concerning consequences of a behavior are viewed as determining attitudes, and normative beliefs are viewed as determining subjective norms, so beliefs about resources and opportunities may be viewed as underlying perceived behavioral control.

Consider the case of regular attendance at class lectures in college. As part of a pilot study, Ajzen and Madden (1986) elicited salient beliefs about factors that might help or interfere with the performance of this behavior. The following ten factors were mentioned with the greatest frequency: conflicting events, sickness, family obligations, employment, being tired or listless, transportation problems, upsetting personal problems, oversleeping or forgetting, heavy load imposed by other classes, and failure to prepare class assignments. In the experiment itself, control beliefs were assessed by asking respondents to rate, on 7-point scales, the likelihood that each of the ten factors would occur. The sum over these responses provided a belief-based measure of perceived behavioral control.

In addition, Ajzen and Madden also asked students to judge more directly how much control they thought they had over regular class attendance. Specifically, the following three questions were posed at separate points in the questionnaire.

1. How much control do you have over whether you do or do not attend this class every session?

complete :__:__:__:__:__:__: very little
control                                            control

2. For me to attend every session of this class is

   easy :__:__:__:__:__:__: difficult

3. If I wanted to, I could easily attend this class every session

   extremely :__:__:__:__:__:__: extremely
   likely                                          unlikely

A direct measure of perceived behavioral control was obtained by summing over responses to these three items. A correlation of 0.54 confirmed the hypothesized link between this direct measure and the belief-based measure of perceived behavioral control described above.

The theory of planned behavior is a general model in which the theory of reasoned action represents a special case. As noted earlier, the original model was designed to deal with behaviors over which people have a high degree of volitional control and it assumed that most behaviors of interest in the domains of personality and social psychology fall into the volitional category (see Ajzen and Fishbein, 1980). The theory of planned behavior, however, explicitly recognizes the possibility that many behaviors may not be under complete control, and the concept of perceived behavioral control is added to handle behaviors of this kind. However, when behavioral control approaches its maximum and issues of control are not among an individual's important considerations, then the theory of planned behavior reduces to the theory of reasoned action. In those instances, neither intentions nor actions will be affected appreciably by beliefs about behavioral control and the only remaining dispositions of interest are attitude toward the behavior and subjective norm.

*Prediction of intentions*

Earlier in this chapter we reviewed some of the empirical evidence in support of the theory of reasoned action. Clearly, this evidence is also supportive of those aspects of the theory of planned behavior that overlap with the theory of reasoned action. The theory of planned behavior, however, goes beyond the theory of reasoned action in that it introduces the concept of perceived behavioral control and proposes a direct causal effect of perceived control on intention, an effect not mediated by attitude or subjective norm. Evidence for this aspect of the theory is examined in the present section.

Schifter and Ajzen (1985) applied the theory of planned behavior to the prediction of weight loss intentions, and actual weight reduction, among female college students. Attitudes toward losing weight during the following 6 weeks were assessed by means of several evaluative semantic differential scales. To measure subjective norms, participants were asked to indicate, again on 7-point scales, whether people who were important to them thought they should lose weight over the next 6 weeks, and whether those people would approve or disapprove of their losing weight. As a measure of perceived behavioral control, participants indicated, on a scale from 0 to 100, the likelihood that if they tried they would manage to reduce their weight over the next 6 weeks and their estimates that an attempt on their part to lose weight would be successful. The final measure of interest for present purposes dealt with intentions to lose weight over the following 6 weeks. Each woman indicated, on several 7-point scales, her intention to try to reduce weight and the intensity of her decision.

The first row in Table 6.7 shows the correlations of intentions to lose weight with attitudes, subjective norms and perceived behavioral control. It can be seen that all three predictors correlated significantly with intention. A hierarchical regression analysis was performed on intentions to lose weight in which attitudes and subjective norms were entered on the first step, and perceived behavioral control on the second.[2] This analysis reveals the effect of perceived behavioral control on intentions after the effects of attitude and subjective norm have been statistically removed. Thus, the hierarchical regression analysis tests the idea that perceived behavioral control contributes to intentions over and above the influence of the two factors contained in the original theory of reasoned action. The results of the analysis confirmed the importance of perceived behavioral control as a third determinant of intentions to lose weight. Although the multiple correlation of intentions with attitudes and subjective norms alone was quite high ($r = 0.65$), it increased significantly – to $0.72$ – with the addition of perceived behavioral control. All three independent variables had significant regression coefficients, indicating that each made an independent contribution to the prediction of weight loss intentions.

The importance of perceived control over a behavioral goal has also been demonstrated in the context of scholastic performance

*Table 6.7*   Correlations of intention (*I*) with attitude toward the behavior
($A_B$), subjective norm (*SN*) and perceived behavioral control
(*PBC*)

| Behavioral goal | $A_B - I$ | $SN - I$ | $PBC - I$ |
|---|---|---|---|
| Losing weight | $0.62^a$ | $0.44^a$ | $0.36^a$ |
| Getting an "A" | $0.48^a$ | $0.11$ | $0.44^a$ |
| Attending class | $0.51^a$ | $0.35^a$ | $0.57^a$ |

[a] Significant at $P < 0.05$.

(Ajzen and Madden, 1986). In one part of the investigation, undergraduate college students enrolled in upper division courses expressed, at the beginning of the semester, their intentions to attempt
getting an "A" grade in the course, as well as their attitudes,
subjective norms and perceived control over this behavioral goal.
Attitudes toward getting an "A," subjective norms, and perceived
behavioral control were each assessed by means of several direct
questions and on the basis of a set of relevant salient beliefs. The
measure of intention was a set of three direct questions dealing with
intentions to try to get an "A."

Before turning to the prediction of intentions it is worth noting
that the study provided support for the hypothesized relation between direct and belief-based measures of attitude, subjective norm,
and perceived behavioral control. The correlations between the two
types of measures ranged from 0.47 to 0.57 ($P < 0.01$).

The second row in Table 6.7 shows the correlations of intentions to
get an "A" with the direct measures of attitudes, subjective norms,
and perceived behavioral control. A hierarchical regression analysis
revealed that attitudes and perceived behavioral control each had a
significant effect on intention. On the basis of attitude toward the
behavior and subjective norm alone, the multiple correlation with
intention was 0.48 ($P < 0.01$). The introduction of perceived behavioral control on the second step of the regression analysis raised
the multiple correlation significantly to the level of 0.65.

Losing weight and getting an "A" in a course are both behavioral
goals over which people clearly have only limited volitional control.
In addition to the desire to lose weight, people have to be familiar
with an appropriate diet or exercise regimen, and they have to be
capable of adhering to the diet or exercise program in the face of
distractions and temptations. Similarly, getting an "A" in a course
depends not only on strong motivation but also on intellectual

ability, availability of sufficient time for study, resisting temptations to engage in activities more attractive than studying, and so on. It is not surprising, therefore, that perceived behavioral control is found to influence intentions to pursue or not to pursue these behavioral goals.

There is also evidence, however, that even when problems of volitional control are much less apparent, people's intentions are affected by their control beliefs. In the investigation by Ajzen and Madden (1986) records were kept of students' attendance of eight class lectures following administration of a questionnaire. The questionnaire contained measures of intention to attend classes regularly, attitudes toward this behavior, subjective norms, and perceived behavioral control. The latter three variables were again assessed by means of direct questions and, more indirectly, on the basis of sets of salient beliefs. The correlations between the belief indices and the direct measures were significant, ranging from 0.47 to 0.54 ($P <$ 0.01). As to the prediction of intentions from the direct measures, in the third row of Table 6.7 it can be seen that perceived behavioral control correlated significantly with intentions, as did attitudes and subjective norms. A hierarchical regression analysis showed that on the basis of attitudes and subjective norms alone, the multiple correlation with intentions was 0.55 ($P < 0.01$). However, the addition of perceived behavioral control on the second step improved the prediction significantly, resulting in a multiple correlation of 0.68.

The findings presented up to this point indicate that the original theory of reasoned action, with its implication that perceived behavioral control can influence intention only indirectly via attitude or subjective norms, is not sufficient. The addition of perceived behavioral control as a direct determinant of intention improved prediction of several behaviors, and this effect was independent of attitudes and subjective norms.[3]

### Prediction of goal attainment

The theory of planned behavior also suggests the possibility that perceived behavioral control may be related to behavior not only indirectly, via its effect on intentions, but also directly, over and above the effect due to intentions. This possibility was explored in the studies described above in which attempts were made to predict attainment of three behavioral goals: attending lectures on a regular

*Table 6.8*    Prediction of behavioral attainment (B) from intention (I) and
perceived behavioral control (PBC)

| Behavioral goal | I − B | PBC − B |
|---|---|---|
| Attending class | 0.36[a] | 0.28[a] |
| Losing weight | 0.25[a] | 0.41[a] |
| Getting an "A" | | |
| beginning of semester | 0.26[a] | 0.11 |
| end of semester | 0.39[a] | 0.38[a] |

[a] Significant at P < 0.05.

basis, getting an "A" in a course, and losing weight. Table 6.8 shows
the correlations between intentions and perceived behavioral control
on the one hand and attainment of the behavioral goal on the other.

With respect to regular class attendance, both intentions and
perceived control correlated significantly with actual behavior. A
hierarchical regression analysis, however, showed that the addition
of perceived behavioral control did not improve prediction of behavior significantly. This was expected since class attendance is a
behavior over which students have considerable volitional control.
The addition of a (subjective) measure of control thus added little
information of value in the prediction of actual behavior.

In contrast, losing weight does pose problems of volitional control. As would therefore be expected, the results with respect to
attainment of this goal showed the relevance of perceived behavioral
control quite dramatically. As can be seen in the second row of Table
6.8, both intentions and perceived control correlated significantly
with goal attainment, but perceived control was the better predictor
of the two. The addition of perceived behavioral control on the
second step of a hierarchical regression analysis improved prediction
significantly, raising the multiple correlation with goal attainment
from 0.25 to 0.44.

Perhaps the most interesting results, however, emerged in the
study on getting an "A" in a course. The questionnaire assessing the
different constructs of the theory of planned behavior was administered twice, once at the beginning of the semester and again toward
the end. Perception of control over getting an "A" should, of course,
become more accurate as the end of the semester approaches. As an
addition to intentions, the later measure of perceived behavioral
control should therefore contribute to the prediction of course
grades more than the earlier measure. The data presented in the last

two rows of Table 6.8 lend support to this hypothesis. Although both measures, intentions and perceived control, gained in predictive accuracy, the more dramatic gain was observed with respect to the latter. Moreover, hierarchical regression analysis showed that whereas with the data obtained early in the semester, only intentions had a significant effect on behavior, with the later data, both intentions and perceived behavioral control had significant regression coefficients. Thus, the addition of perceived behavioral control had no effect on the accuracy of behavioral prediction for the data obtained early in the semester, but it raised the correlation significantly from 0.39 to 0.45 for the data obtained toward the end of the semester.[4]

Before concluding this discussion it may be instructive to take a closer look at the way in which the examination of control beliefs can aid our understanding of the factors that determine behavioral performance. We shall use academic achievement as an example. This analysis parallels our earlier discussion of behavioral and normative beliefs as determinants of a mother's choice to breast-feed or bottle-feed her baby. In a pilot study conducted prior to the main experiment, Ajzen and Madden (1986) asked college students to list any factors that could help them get an "A" in a course and any factors that might make it difficult for them to get an "A." Four potential facilitating factors mentioned frequently were stimulating subject matter, clear and organized lectures, possession of required skills and background, and availability of help from the instructor. Four frequently mentioned factors whose presence would hamper attaining a good grade were taking other demanding classes, extracurricular activities, arduous text and reading materials, and difficult exams and course requirements. In the second wave of the main experiment, toward the end of the semester, college students were asked to judge, with respect to each of these eight factors, how much the factor was likely to influence their ability to get an "A" in a particular course they were taking at the time.

Table 6.9 shows the average control beliefs scored in the direction of facilitation (1 = factor hinders attaining a good grade, 7 = factor facilitates attaining a good grade) as well as the correlation of each belief with the intention to get an "A" and with actual grades attained. Inspection of the mean control beliefs reveals that the students who took part in the experiment thought they would be helped by the subject matter of the course which was stimulating enough to motivate them, by the lectures which they considered to be

*Table 6.9*    Mean control beliefs and correlations with intentions and
            attained grades

|  |  | Correlation with | |
| --- | --- | --- | --- |
| *Control beliefs* | *Mean* | *Intention* | *Grade* |
| *Facilitating factors* | | | |
| Stimulating subject matter | 5.19 | 0.50 | 0.37 |
| Clear and organized lectures | 5.37 | 0.33 | 0.35 |
| Possession of skills and background | 5.11 | 0.44 | 0.45 |
| Availability of help | 6.17 | 0.21 | 0.31 |
| *Obstructing factors* | | | |
| Other demanding classes | 2.41 | 0.24 | 0.27 |
| Extracurricular activities | 2.67 | 0.19 | 0.19 |
| Arduous text and reading materials | 4.17 | 0.11[a] | 0.16[a] |
| Exams and course requirements | 3.16 | 0.33 | 0.35 |

[a] Not significant; all other correlations $P < 0.05$.

sufficiently clear and organized, by their possessing the required
skills and background, and by the ready availability of help from the
instructor. On the other hand, the students also believed that they
would encounter certain obstacles, especially in the form of demands
on their time and energy imposed by other classes they were taking
and in the form of extracurricular activities.

The correlations displayed in Table 6.9 demonstrate the impact of
these different control beliefs on intentions to make an effort to get
an "A" in the course and on actual grades attained. Of special
importance were perceptions concerning the course's subject matter,
lecture organization, possession of required skills and background,
and the nature of the exams and other course requirements. The
more that students saw these factors as facilitating their performance
in the course, the stronger were their intentions to try for an "A" and
the higher were the grades they actually attained.

In conclusion, the experiments reviewed above have provided
some initial support for the theory of planned behavior. The addition
of perceived behavioral control to the variables contained in the
original theory of reasoned action was found greatly to improve the
prediction of behavioral intentions. This finding indicates that
perception of behavioral control, like attitude toward the behavior
and subjective norm, can have an important impact on a person's
behavioral motivation. The more that attainment of a behavioral
goal is viewed as being under volitional control, the stronger is the

person's intention to try. In addition, perceived behavioral control can also improve the prediction of actual behavior beyond the level obtained on the basis of intentions alone. This is the case, however, only under certain conditions. First, the behavior must at least in part be determined by factors beyond a person's control. When the behavior is largely under volitional control, intentions alone are found to be sufficient to predict it. Secondly, perceived behavioral control must be fairly realistic, reflecting actual control to a reasonable degree. This condition was apparently met in the study on weight loss, and it was also fulfilled toward the end of the semester in the study on academic performance.

## Summary and conclusions

This chapter discussed a theoretical framework, the theory of planned behavior, that can help us predict and understand the performance of specific action tendencies. We examined some of the factors that influence deliberate performance of willful actions as well as additional factors that must be taken into account when we are dealing with behaviors or behavioral goals over which people have only limited volitional control. We saw that volitional control is best defined as a continuum, where the ideal case at one extreme is represented by purely volitional acts and the ideal case at the other extreme are behavioral events which are completely beyond volitional control. Most behaviors, however, fall somewhere between these extremes. Toward the volitional side of the continuum, it is possible to predict behavior with a great deal of accuracy on the basis of intentions to perform the behavior in question. Intentions also contribute to the attainment of behavioral goals that are only partly under volitional control; here, however, their predictive validity is attenuated and we must take account of factors that can interfere with or facilitate performance of the intended behavior. Perceived behavioral control can reflect the presence of such factors and, to the extent that it does so accurately, contributes to the prediction of behavioral achievement.

Perceived behavioral control can also have motivational implications, influencing the formation of behavioral intentions. When resources or opportunities are seen as inadequate, motivation to try performing the behavior is likely to suffer. In addition to being affected by perceived behavioral control, intentions are also influenced by attitudes toward the behavior and by subjective norms. Generally speaking, then, people intend to perform a behavior if their personal evaluations of it are favorable, if they think that important others would approve of it, and if they believe that the requisite resources and opportunities will be available. To some extent, strength in one factor can compensate for weakness in another. People who doubt their ability to carry out a certain behavioral plan may nevertheless intend to make a serious effort if they place a high positive value on performing the behavior or if they experience strong social pressure to do so.

Substantive knowledge about the determinants of specific action tendencies is obtained by examining the informational foundation of attitudes, subjective norms, and perceived behavioral control. Beliefs concerning the likely outcomes of a behavior, and subjective evaluations of those outcomes, reveal why a person holds a favorable or unfavorable attitude toward performing the behavior; beliefs about the normative expectations of salient referent individuals or groups, and motivations to comply with these referents, provide an understanding of perceived social pressure to perform or not perform the behavior; and beliefs concerning factors that can prevent or facilitate goal attainment disclose the considerations that produce perceptions of high or low behavioral control. Taken together, this informational base provides us with a detailed explanation of a person's tendency to perform, or not to perform, a particular behavior.

## Notes

1. Factors further removed from the behavior, such as a person's demographic characteristics, personality traits, or global attitudes toward the target of the behavior, are assumed to have no direct impact on behavioral performance. According to the theory of reasoned action, variables of this kind will be related to behavior if, and only if, they influence the beliefs that underlie the behavior's attitudinal or normative determinants.

2. The data in these studies were also analyzed by means of LISREL (Jöreskog and Sörbom, 1983), where the direct and indirect measures served as different indicators of attitude, subjective norm, and perceived behavioral control. The results obtained were very similar to those reported here.

3. The addition of interaction terms involving perceived behavioral control and the other two independent variables (attitudes and subjective norms) did not significantly improve the prediction of intentions.

4. The interaction between perceived behavioral control and intentions, when added to the prediction equation, did not have a significant effect on goal attainment.

## Suggestions for further readings

1. Ajzen, I. and Fishbein, M. (1980). *Understanding attitudes and predicting social behavior*. Englewood-Cliffs, NJ: Prentice-Hall. This book is a low-level introduction to the theory of reasoned action and also provides several applied illustrations that show how the theory can be used to further prediction and understanding of behaviors in different domains.
2. Kuhl, J. and Beckmann, J. (Eds) (1985). *Action-control: From cognition to behavior*. Heidelberg: Springer. In this book, several theorists present their ideas on the problems of volitional control over behavior and the factors that may interfere with such control.

# 7 / CONCLUSION

People carry within them the accumulated experiences of countless prior generations handed down in the form of genetic endowment, as well as the outcomes of their own unique life histories. Genetic differences and divergent personal experiences ensure that no two individuals are exactly alike. It is hardly surprising that attempts to understand human behavior have proved to be as frustrating as they are challenging. The historical processes and events that have shaped a person's complex make-up can never be fully unraveled. Nevertheless, our task is not hopeless. A person's current behavior must be determined by factors that exert their effects right here and now. Past events are important only to the extent that they have left an enduring mark on the person, a mark that continues to wield its impact. As Campbell (1963) has pointed out, attitudes and personality traits are meant to capture these residues of past experience. By assessing attitudes or personality traits we attempt to unveil the hidden factors that, as a result of past events, have come to predispose an individual to act in certain ways.

We have learned a great deal in recent years about the nature of these behavioral dispositions. No longer do we hear calls for abandoning the trait approach in personality or for dispensing with the attitude construct. It is now generally understood that there is no magic about trait or attitude measures. We cannot construct a broad personality inventory or attitude scale and hope to use it as a basis for the prediction and explanation of any conceivable behavioral criterion. In fact, the very distinction between, on the one hand, attitudes and personality traits assessed by means of a questionnaire, and, on the other hand, "overt" or objective behavior must be discarded.

Even so-called overt actions, observed and recorded by trained investigators, are usually of little interest in and of themselves. We rarely attempt to predict or explain single acts performed under a unique set of circumstances. Instead, behavioral observations normally serve as indicators of people's more general response tendencies; that is, of their behavioral dispositions. Whether responses used to infer a disposition are verbal or nonverbal, obtained by means of a questionnaire, observation of behavior, self-reports, or peer reports is largely immaterial. Depending on circumstances, one means of data collection may produce more valid measures than another, but there is no difference in principle. Each of these methods can be used to infer the underlying disposition of interest.

It has also become very clear that response dispositions can be defined and measured at various levels of generality or specificity. Aggregation of responses across time, contexts, targets, or actions – or across a combination of these elements – permits inferences of dispositions at varying levels of generality. Inferred dispositions can range from the tendency to perform a single action (over time) to the tendency to engage in a broad range of actions, as reflected in a multiple-act aggregate. Even when they address the same content domain, two measures can be considered indicators of the *same* disposition only if they correspond in their levels of generality. And it is only in the presence of such compatibility that behavioral consistencies manifest themselves reliably. The realization that measures of global attitudes and personality traits, obtained by means of responses to questionnaires, are compatible only with equally general, broadly aggregated measures of other types of responses has helped to clarify much of the initially baffling lack of predictive validity.

It is no longer very meaningful to ask whether attitudes and personality traits predict behavior. Nor does the crucial issue have to do with the conditions under which attitudes and personality traits are related to behavior. Instead, the literature poses and provides answers to three interrelated questions. First, is there consistency between different observations of behavior? Secondly, are general behavioral dispositions related to specific response tendencies? Finally, do verbal responses predict nonverbal behavior?

*Behavioral consistency.* The answer to the question of behavioral consistency across observations is closely tied to the principle of aggregation. Generally speaking, observations of single actions on individual occasions do not correlate well with each other. Too many factors unique to a given occasion prevent emergence of a clear response tendency. However, by aggregating observations of a given behavior across occasions we obtain a stable measure of the disposition to perform the behavior in question. Temporal stability is in fact found to become quite high with aggregation over a sufficient number of observations.

There is also evidence for consistency between behavioral measures that aggregate across different actions, so long as each aggregate assesses the same broad underlying disposition. We can infer broad dispositions from representative samples of behaviors performed in a variety of situations, and multiple measures of this kind tend to correlate highly with each other.

The aggregation solution to the consistency dilemma of course limits the explanatory and predictive utilities of traits and attitudes to broad classes of responses; it does not provide a means for the prediction of tendencies to engage in specific behaviors. This limitation, however, is perhaps of more concern in applied attitude research, where the aim often is to predict specific actions, than it is in personality research which deals largely with broad response tendencies. The principle of compatibility overcomes the limitation in the attitude domain by permitting attitudes to be reduced to the level of individual behaviors.

*General dispositions and specific actions.* As a general rule, broad response dispositions are poor predictors of specific actions. This is perhaps the most important lesson to be learned from the prolonged consistency controversy, but also perhaps the most difficult to accept. It would indeed be very convenient if we could measure general attitudes or personality traits and use the resulting scores to predict any behavior that appears relevant to the disposition in question. Unfortunately, both theory and empirical findings negate this possibility.

The alternative attempt to link broad behavioral dispositions to specific response tendencies by means of moderating variables has produced some interesting studies, but future progress along these lines faces serious difficulties. Perhaps the greatest shortcoming of the moderating variables approach at this point is the lack of a conceptual framework, or even of a taxonomy, of the personal, situational, and behavioral factors that can be expected to interact with dispositions in the determination of specific actions (see Kenrick and Dantchik, 1983; Magnusson, 1981). An encouraging step in the direction of developing an integrative conceptual framework has been taken by Fazio (1986; Fazio *et al.*, 1982, 1983) in his work on attitude accessibility. However, this framework is, at this stage, largely limited to the moderating effects of such variables as involvement with the attitude object, confidence in one's attitude, and direct experience in the attitudinal domain.

Even if a more general framework were to emerge, there is no assurance that the moderating variables identified would indeed be found to affect accuracy of prediction in a consistent manner, or that they would not interact with still other factors to produce a maze of difficult to reconcile effects. In any event, the multitude of conditions that moderating variables place on the prediction of specific responses from broad dispositions severely limits the practical utility of this approach.

*Verbal and nonverbal responses.* What people say and what they do are not always the same (Deutscher, 1966, 1973). In part, this is a problem of measurement validity. The validity of verbal responses has often been questioned because of the possible presence of social desirability biases, acquiescence tendencies, strategic biases, and so forth. Somewhat less attention has been given to the measurement implications of the fact that observed actions may be equally biased to create favorable impressions, to avoid conflict, or to gain an advantage by means of ingratiation. The consequence of such biases is to invalidate the measures from which behavioral dispositions are inferred. If the biases associated with a verbal response differ greatly from the biases operating on the physical action, correlations between the two measures will necessarily deteriorate.

The potential for biased responding does not, however, doom efforts to predict nonverbal from verbal behaviors. Many situations provide little incentive for strong biases, and tendencies toward biased responding can be further reduced by the careful application of appropriate measurement procedures. The question therefore remains, what is the relation between valid, relatively nonbiased verbal and nonverbal responses? The answer to this question is related to the principle of compatibility, and it has nothing to do with the fact that one indicator of the disposition is verbal and the other nonverbal. Instead, the answer revolves around the generality or specificity of the measures involved. As noted above, verbal measures of broad attitudes or personality traits have been shown to predict equally broad, multiple-act measures of overt behavior. However, as a general rule, they do not predict specific responses, whether nonverbal or verbal. To predict single actions, we must turn to dispositional measures that deal specifically with those actions. The concept of intention appears to be a useful starting point. Intentions represent behavioral dispositions that conceptually are very closely tied to the corresponding behavior, and there is good evidence that many behaviors are sufficiently under volitional control to be predictable from people's intentions. Barring unforeseen events, people tend to carry out their behavioral plans. Added difficulties arise when the achievement of a behavioral goal is at least partly determined by internal or external factors over which a person has only limited control. The theory of planned behavior described in Chapter 6 represents an attempt to account for the formation of intentions and the achievement of behavioral goals. Attitudes toward the behavior, subjective norms, and perceived behavioral control are the three primary determinants of intentions. Their formation is traced, respectively, to beliefs about the behavior's likely outcomes, beliefs about the expectations of important others, and beliefs about factors that may facilitate or hinder performance of the behavior. When people are aware of potential difficulties, they are assumed to plan their actions accordingly. The theory of planned behavior is thus designed to permit prediction and explanation of behavioral achievement by taking into account motivational antecedents, reflected in intentions, as well as other factors that are only partly under volitional control, factors that are reflected in perceived behavioral control.

This book ends the way it began, with the dispositional prediction of human behavior. It should be clear by now that dispositional concepts are not only useful, they are indispensable tools at the disposal of the behavioral scientist. While measures of behavioral dispositions cannot be used indiscriminately, when appropriately employed they yield highly valuable information. As intuitive observation would suggest, people are quite consistent in the patterns of behavior they exhibit. They act in ways that cannot be described as capricious, nor would it be accurate to claim that their behavior is controlled by external forces. Instead, human action is found to follow reasonably and consistently from relevant behavioral dispositions.

# REFERENCES

Abelson, R. P., Aronson, E., McGuire, W. J., Newcomb, T. M., Rosenberg, M. J. and Tannenbaum, P. H. (Eds) (1968). *Theories of cognitive consistency: A sourcebook.* Chicago: Rand McNally.

Ajzen, I. (1971). Attitudinal vs. normative messages: An investigation of the differential effects of persuasive communications on behavior. *Sociometry*, 34, 263–80.

Ajzen, I. (1982). On behaving in accordance with one's attitudes. In M. P. Zanna, E. T. Higgins and C. P. Herman (Eds), *Consistency in social behavior: The Ontario Symposium*, Vol. 2, pp. 3–15. Hillsdale, NJ: Lawrence Erlbaum Associates.

Ajzen, I. (1985). From intentions to actions: A theory of planned behavior. In J. Kuhl and J. Beckmann (Eds), *Action-control: From cognition to behavior*, pp. 11–39. Heidelberg: Springer.

Ajzen, I. (1987). Attitudes, traits, and actions: Dispositional prediction of behavior in personality and social psychology. In L. Berkowitz (Ed.), *Advances in experimental social psychology*, Vol. 20. San Diego: Academic Press.

Ajzen, I. and Fishbein, M. (1970). The prediction of behavior from attitudinal and normative variables. *Journal of Experimental Social Psychology*, 6, 466–87.

Ajzen, I. and Fishbein, M. (1977). Attitude–behavior relations: A theoretical analysis and review of empirical research. *Psychological Bulletin*, 84, 888–918.

Ajzen, I. and Fishbein, M. (1980). *Understanding attitudes and predicting social behavior.* Englewood-Cliffs, NJ: Prentice-Hall.

Ajzen, I. and Madden, T. J. (1986). Prediction of goal-directed behavior: Attitudes, intentions, and perceived behavioral control. *Journal of Experimental Social Psychology*, 22, 453–74.

Ajzen, I. and Timko, C. (1986). Correspondence between health attitudes and behavior. *Journal of Basic and Applied Social Psychology*, 7, 259–76.

Ajzen, I., Timko, C. and White, J. B. (1982). Self-monitoring and the attitude–behavior relation. *Journal of Personality and Social Psychology*, 42, 426–35.

Alagna, S. W. and Reddy, D. M. (1984). Predictors of proficient technique and successful lesion detection in breast self-examination. *Health Psychology*, 3, 113–27.

Allport, G. W. (1935). Attitudes. In C. Murchinson (Ed.), *A handbook of social psychology*, pp. 798–844. Worcester, MA: Clark University Press.

Allport, G. W. (1937). *Personality: A psychological interpretation*. New York: Holt.

Allport, G. W. (1954). The historical background of modern social psychology. In G. Lindzey (Ed.), *Handbook of social psychology*, Vol. 1, pp. 3–56. Cambridge, MA: Addison-Wesley.

Allport, G. W. (1961). *Patterns and growth in personality*. New York: Holt.

Bagozzi, R. P. (1978). The construct validity of the affective, behavioral, and cognitive components of attitude by analysis of covariance structures. *Multivariate Behavioral Research*, 13, 9–31.

Bagozzi, R. P. and Burnkrant, R. E. (1979). Attitude organization and the attitude–behavior relationship. *Journal of Personality and Social Psychology*, 37, 913–29.

Bagozzi, R. P. and Burnkrant, R. E. (1985). Attitude organization and the attitude–behavior relation: A reply to Dillon and Kumar. *Journal of Personality and Social Psychology*, 49, 47–57.

Bandura, A. (1977). Self-efficacy: Toward a unifying theory of behavioral change. *Psychological Review*, 84, 191–215.

Bandura, A. (1982). Self-efficacy mechanism in human agency. *American Psychologist*, 37, 122–47.

Bandura, A., Blanchard, E. B. and Ritter, B. (1969). Relative efficacy of desensitization and modeling approaches for inducing behavioral, affective, and attitudinal changes. *Journal of Personality and Social Psychology*, 13, 173–99.

Bandura, A., Adams, N. E. and Beyer, J. (1977). Cognitive processes mediating behavioral change. *Journal of Personality and Social Psychology*, 35, 125–39.

Baron, R. M. and Kenny, D. A. (1986). The moderator–mediator variable distinction in social psychological research: Conceptual, strategic, and statistical considerations. *Journal of Personality and Social Psychology*, 51, 1173–82.

Bar-Tal, D. and Bar-Zohar, Y. (1977). The relationship between perception of locus of control and academic achievement. *Contemporary Educational Psychology*, 2, 181–99.

Bauman, K. C. and Dent, C. W. (1982). The influence of an objective measure on self-reports of behavior. *Journal of Applied Psychology*, **67**, 623–8.

Becherer, R. C. and Richard, L. M. (1978). Self-monitoring as a moderating variable in consumer behavior. *Journal of Consumer Research*, **5**, 159–62.

Bem, D. J. (1965). An experimental analysis of self persuasion. *Journal of Experimental Social Psychology*, **1**, 199–218.

Bem, D. J. (1970). *Beliefs, attitudes and human affairs*. Belmont, CA: Brooks/Cole.

Bem, D. J. and Allen, A. (1974). On predicting some of the people some of the time: The search for cross-situational consistencies in behavior. *Psychological Review*, **81**, 506–20.

Blass, T. (1984). Social psychology and personality: Toward a convergence. *Journal of Personality and Social Psychology*, **47**, 1013–27.

Bowers, K. S. (1973). Interactionism in psychology: An analysis and critique. *Psychological Review*, **80**, 307–36.

Breckler, S. J. (1984). Empirical validation of affect, behavior, and cognition as distinct components of attitude. *Journal of Personality and Social Psychology*, **47**, 1191–1205.

Brown, D. W. (1974). Adolescent attitudes and lawful behavior. *Public Opinion Quarterly*, **38**, 98–106.

Buss, A. H. (1961). *The psychology of aggression*. New York: Wiley.

Buss, A. H. (1980). *Self-consciousness and social anxiety*. San Francisco: W. H. Freeman.

Buss, D. M. and Craik, K. H. (1980). The frequency concept of disposition: Dominance and prototypically dominant acts. *Journal of Personality*, **48**, 379–92.

Buss, D. M. and Craik, K. H. (1981). The act frequency analysis of interpersonal dispositions: Aloofness, gregariousness, dominance, and submissiveness. *Journal of Personality*, **49**, 174–92.

Buss, D. M. and Craik, K. H. (1984). Acts, dispositions, and personality. In B. A. Maher and W. B. Maher (Eds), *Progress in experimental personality research*, pp. 241–301. San Diego: Academic Press.

Cacioppo, J. T., Petty, R. E., Kao, C. F. and Rodriguez, R. (1986a). Central and peripheral routes to persuasion: An individual difference perspective. *Journal of Personality and Social Psychology*, **51**, 1032–43.

Cacioppo, J. T., Petty, R. E., Losch, M. E. and Kim, H. S. (1986b). Electromyographic activity over facial muscle regions can differentiate the valence and intensity of affective reactions. *Journal of Personality and Social Psychology*, **50**, 260–8.

Campbell, A., Converse, P. E., Miller, W. E. and Stokes, D. E. (1960). *The American voter*. New York: Wiley.

Campbell, D. T. (1963). Social attitudes and other acquired behavioral dispositions. In S. Koch (Ed.), *Psychology: A study of a science*, Vol. 6, pp. 94–172. New York: McGraw-Hill.

Carver, C. S. (1975). Physical aggression as a function of objective self-awareness and attitude toward punishment. *Journal of Experimental Social Psychology*, **11**, 510–19.

Carver, C. S. and Scheier, M. F. (1981). *Attention and self-regulation: A control-theory approach to human behavior*. New York: Springer.

Cattell, R. B. (1946). *Description and measurement of personality*. Yonkers-on-Hudson, NY: World Book Co.

Cattell, R. B. (1947). Confirmation and clarification of the primary personality factors. *Psychometrika*, **12**, 197–220.

Chaiken, S. and Yates, S. (1985). Affective-cognitive consistency and thought-induced attitude polarization. *Journal of Personality and Social Psychology*, **49**, 1470–81.

Chaplin, W. F. and Goldberg, L. R. (1984). A failure to replicate the Bem and Allen study of individual differences in cross-situational consistency. *Journal of Personality and Social Psychology*, **47**, 1074–90.

Cohen, A. R., Stotland, E. and Wolfe, D. M. (1955). An experimental investigation of need for cognition. *Journal of Abnormal and Social Psychology*, **51**, 291–4.

Cohen, J. (1978). Partialed products *are* interactions; partialed powers *are* curve components. *Psychological Bulletin*, **85**, 858–66.

Cohen, J. (1983). The cost of dichotomization. *Applied Psychological Measurement*, **7**, 249–53.

Crandall, V. C., Katkovsky, W. and Crandall, V. J. (1965). Children's beliefs in their own control of reinforcement in intellectual-academic situations. *Child Development*, **36**, 91–109.

Cronbach, L. J. (1975). Beyond the two disciplines of scientific psychology. *American Psychologist*, **30**, 116–27.

Davidson, A. R., Yantis, S., Norwood, M. and Montano, D. E. (1985). Amount of information about the attitude object and attitude-behavior consistency. *Journal of Personality and Social Psychology*, **49**, 1184–98.

DeFleur, M. L. and Westie, F. R. (1958). Verbal attitudes and overt acts: An experiment on the salience of attitudes. *American Sociological Review*, **23**, 667–73.

Deutscher, I. (1966). Words and deeds. *Social Problems*, **13**, 235–54.

Deutscher, I. (1973). *What we say/what we do: Sentiments and acts*. Glenview, IL: Scott, Foresman.

Digman, J. M. and Inouye, J. (1986). Further specification of the five robust factors of personality. *Journal of Personality and Social Psychology*, **50**, 116–23.

Dillon, W. R. and Kumar, A. (1985). Attitude organization and the attitude-behavior relation: A critique of Bagozzi and Burnkrant's reanalysis of Fishbein and Ajzen. *Journal of Personality and Social Psychology*, **49**, 33–46.

Drake, R. A. and Sobrero, A. P. (1985). Trait–behavior and attitude–

behavior consistency: Lateral orientation effects. Unpublished manuscript, University of Colorado.

Dudycha, G. J. (1936). An objective study of punctuality in relation to personality and achievement. *Archives of Psychology*, 29, 1–53.

Dulany, D. E. (1968). Awareness, rules, and propositional control: A confrontation with S-R behavior theory. In D. Horton and T. Dixon (Eds), *Verbal behavior and S-R behavior theory*, pp. 340–87. Englewood-Cliffs, NJ: Prentice-Hall.

Duval, S. and Wicklund, R. A. (1972). *A theory of objective self-awareness*. San Diego: Academic Press.

Eagly, A. H. (1974). The comprehensibility of persuasive arguments as a determinant of opinion change. *Journal of Personality and Social Psychology*, 29, 758–73.

Edwards, A. L. (1957). *Techniques of attitude scale construction*. New York: Appleton-Century-Crofts.

Edwards, A. L. and Abbott, R. D. (1973a). Relationship among the EPI scales, the EPPS, and the PRF scales. *Journal of Consulting and Clinical Psychology*, 40, 27–32.

Edwards, A. L. and Abbott, R. D. (1973b). Relationship between the EPI scales and the 16 PF, CPI, and EPPS scales. *Educational and Psychological Measurement*, 33, 231–8.

Edwards, A. L. and Kenney, K. C. (1946). A comparison of the Thurstone and Likert techniques of attitude scale construction. *Journal of Applied Psychology*, 30, 72–83.

Ekehammer, B. (1974). Interactionism in personality from a historical perspective. *Psychological Bulletin*, 81, 1026–48.

Endler, N. S. and Magnusson, D. (1976). Toward an interactional theory of personality. *Psychological Bulletin*, 83, 956–74.

Epstein, S. (1979). The stability of behavior: I. On predicting most of the people much of the time. *Journal of Personality and Social Psychology*, 37, 1097–1126.

Epstein, S. (1980a). The self-concept: A review and the proposal of an integrated theory of personality. In E. Staub (Ed.), *Personality: Basic aspects and current research*, pp. 81–132. Englewood-Cliffs, NJ: Prentice-Hall.

Epstein, S. (1980b). The stability of behavior: II. Implications for psychological research. *American Psychologist*, 35, 790–807.

Epstein, S. (1983a). The unconscious, the preconscious, and the self-concept. In J. Suls and A. Greenwald (Eds), *Psychological perspectives on the self*, Vol. 2, pp. 219–47. Hillsdale, NJ: Lawrence Erlbaum Associates.

Epstein, S. (1983b). Aggregation and beyond: Some basic issues on the prediction of behavior. *Journal of Personality*, 51, 360–92.

Epstein, S. and O'Brien, E. J. (1985). The person-situation debate in historical and current perspective. *Psychological Bulletin*, 98, 513–37.

Evans, D. A. and Alexander, S. (1970). Some psychological correlates of civil rights activity. *Psychological Reports*, 26, 899–906.

Eysenck, H. J. (1947). *Dimensions of personality*. London: Kegan Paul.

Eysenck, H. J. (1953). *The structure of human personality*. New York: Wiley.

Eysenck, H. J. (1956). The questionnaire measurement of neuroticism and extraversion. *Revista de Psicologia*, 50, 113–40.

Eysenck, H. J. (1967). *The biological basis of personality*. Springfield, IL: Charles C. Thomas.

Fazio, R. H. (1986). How do attitudes guide behavior? In R. M. Sorrentino and E. T. Higgins (Eds), *The handbook of motivation and cognition: Foundations of social behavior*, pp. 204–43. New York: Guilford.

Fazio, R. H. and Williams, C. J. (1986). Attitude accessibility as a moderator of the attitude–perception and attitude–behavior relations: An investigation of the 1984 presidential election. *Journal of Personality and Social Psychology*, 51, 505–14.

Fazio, R. H. and Zanna, M. P. (1978a). Attitudinal qualities relating to the strength of the attitude–behavior relationship. *Journal of Experimental Social Psychology*, 14, 398–408.

Fazio, R. H. and Zanna, M. P. (1978b). On the predictive validity of attitudes: The roles of direct experience and confidence. *Journal of Personality*, 46, 228–43.

Fazio, R. H. and Zanna, M. P. (1981). Direct experience and attitude–behavior consistency. In L. Berkowitz (Ed.), *Advances in experimental social psychology*, Vol. 14, pp. 161–202. San Diego: Academic Press.

Fazio, R. H., Chen, J., McDonel, E. C. and Sherman, S. J. (1982). Attitude accessibility, attitude–behavior consistency, and the strength of the object-evaluation association. *Journal of Experimental Social Psychology*, 18, 339–57.

Fazio, R. H., Powell, M. C. and Herr, P. M. (1983). Toward a process model of the attitude–behavior relation: Accessing one's attitude upon mere observation of the attitude object. *Journal of Personality and Social Psychology*, 44, 723–35.

Fenigstein, A., Scheier, M., and Buss, A. (1975). Public and private self-consciousness: Assessment and theory. *Journal of Consulting and Clinical Psychology*, 43, 522–7.

Festinger, L. (1957). *A theory of cognitive dissonance*. Evanston, IL: Row-Peterson.

Fishbein, M. (1963). An investigation of the relationships between beliefs about an object and the attitude toward that object. *Human Relations*, 16, 233–40.

Fishbein, M. and Ajzen, I. (1974). Attitudes toward objects as predictors of single and multiple behavioral criteria. *Psychological Review*, 81, 59–74.

Fishbein, M. and Ajzen, I. (1975). *Belief, attitude, intention, and behavior:*

*An introduction to theory and research.* Reading, MA: Addison-Wesley.

Fishbein, M. and Ajzen, I. (1981). Attitudes and voting behavior: An application of the theory of reasoned action. In G. M. Stephenson and J. M. Davis (Eds), *Progress in applied social psychology*, Vol. 1, pp. 253–313. London: Wiley.

Fishbein, M. and Coombs, F. S. (1974). Basis for decision: An attitudinal analysis of voting behavior. *Journal of Applied Social Psychology*, 4, 95–124.

Fishbein, M., Thomas, K. and Jaccard, J. J. (1976). Voting behavior in Britain: An attitudinal analysis. *Occasional Papers in Survey Research*, 7. SSRC Survey Unit, London.

Fiske, D. W. (1949). Consistency of factorial structures of personality ratings from different sources. *Journal of Abnormal and Social Psychology*, 44, 329–44.

Foa, U. G. (1958). The contiguity principle in the structure of interpersonal relations. *Human Relations*, 11, 229–38.

Froming, W. J., Walker, G. R. and Lopyan, K. J. (1982). Public and private self-awareness: When personal attitudes conflict with societal expectations. *Journal of Experimental Social Psychology*, 18, 476–87.

Funder, D. C., Block, J. H. and Block, J. (1983). Delay of gratification: Some longitudinal personality correlates. *Journal of Personality and Social Psychology*, 44, 1198–1213.

Gibb, C. A. (1969). Leadership. In G. Lindzey and E. Aronson (Eds), *Handbook of social psychology*, 2nd edition, Vol. 4, pp. 205–82. Reading, MA: Addison-Wesley.

Gore, P. S. and Rotter, J. B. (1963). A personality correlate of social action. *Journal of Personality*, 31, 58–64.

Gough, H. G. (1957). *Manual for the California Psychological Inventory*. Palo Alto, CA: Consulting Psychologists Press.

Green, B. F. (1954). Attitude measurement. In G. Lindzey (Ed.), *Handbook of social psychology*, Vol. 1, pp. 335–69. Reading, MA: Addison-Wesley.

Guttman, L. (1955). An outline of some new methodology for social research. *Public Opinion Quarterly*, 18, 395–404.

Guttman, L. (1957). Introduction to facet design and analysis. *Proceedings of the Fifteenth International Congress of Psychology*, Brussels, pp. 130–2. Amsterdam: North-Holland.

Guttman, L. (1959). A structural theory for intergroup beliefs and action. *American Sociological Review*, 24, 318–28.

Hall, S. M. and Hall, R. G. (1974). Outcome and methodological considerations in behavioral treatment of obesity. *Behavioral Therapy*, 5, 352–64.

Hartshorne, H. and May, M. A. (1928). *Studies in the nature of character: Vol. 1. Studies in deceit*. New York: Macmillan.

ATTITUDES, PERSONALITY, AND BEHAVIOR

Hartshorne, H., May, M. A. and Maller, J. B. (1929). *Studies in the nature of character: Vol. 2. Studies in self-control*. New York: Macmillan.
Hartshorne, H., May, M. A. and Shuttleworth, F. K. (1930). *Studies in the nature of character: Vol. 3. Studies in the organization of character*. New York: Macmillan.
Heider, F. (1944). Social perception and phenomenal causality. *Psychological Review*, 51, 358–74.
Heider, F. (1958). *The psychology of interpersonal relations*. New York: Wiley.
Hilgard, E. R. (1980). The trilogy of mind: Cognition, affection, and conation. *Journal of the History of the Behavioral Sciences*, 16, 107–17.
Hill, R. J. (1981). Attitudes and behavior. In M. Rosenberg and R. H. Turner (Eds), *Social psychology: Sociological perspectives*, pp. 347–77. New York: Basic Books.
Himmelstein, P. and Moore, J. C. (1963). Racial attitudes and the action of Negro- and white-background figures as factors in petition signing. *Journal of Social Psychology*, 61, 267–72.
Isen, A. M. and Levin, P. F. (1972). Effect of feeling good on helping: Cookies and kindness. *Journal of Personality and Social Psychology*, 21, 384–8.
Jaccard, J. J. (1974). Predicting social behavior from personality traits. *Journal of Research in Personality*, 7, 358–67.
Jackson, D. N. (1967). *Personality research form manual*. Goshen, NY: Research Psychologists Press.
Jackson, D. N. (1971). The dynamics of structured personality tests: 1971. *Psychological Review*, 78, 229–48.
Jackson, D. N. and Paunonen, S. V. (1985). Construct validity and the predictability of behavior. *Journal of Personality and Social Psychology*, 49, 554–70.
Jessor, R. and Jessor, S. (1977). *Problem behavior and psychosocial development*. San Diego: Academic Press.
Jones, E. E. and Davis, K. E. (1965). From acts to dispositions: The attribution process in person perception. In L. Berkowitz (Ed.), *Advances in experimental social psychology*, Vol. 2, pp. 219–66. San Diego: Academic Press.
Jones, E. E. and Sigall, H. (1971). The bogus pipeline: A new paradigm for measuring affect and attitude. *Psychological Bulletin*, 76, 349–64.
Jöreskog, K. G. and Sörbom, D. (1983). *LISREL VI: Estimation of linear structural equation systems by maximum likelihood methods*. Chicago: National Educational Resources.
Katz, D. and Stotland, E. (1959). A preliminary statement of a theory of attitude structure and change. In S. Koch (Ed.), *Psychology: A study of a science*, Vol. 3, pp. 423–75. New York: McGraw-Hill.

Kelley, H. H. (1971). *Attribution in social interaction*. New York: General Learning Press.

Kelly, G. A. (1955). *The psychology of personal constructs*, 2 volumes. New York: Norton.

Kenrick, D. T. and Dantchik, A. (1983). Interactionism, idiographics, and the social psychological invasion of personality. *Journal of Personality*, **51**, 286–307.

King, G. W. (1975). An analysis of attitudinal and normative variables as predictors of intentions and behavior. *Speech Monographs*, **42**, 237–44.

Kirkpatrick, C. (1949). Religion and humanitarianism: A study of institutional implications. *Psychological Monographs*, **63**, 191 (Whole No. 304).

Kleinmuntz, B. (1967). *Personality measurement: An introduction*. Homewood, IL: Dorsey.

Knapper, C. K. and Cropley, A. J. (1981). Social and interpersonal factors in driving. In G. M. Stephenson and J. H. Davis (Eds), *Progress in applied social psychology*, Vol. 1, pp. 191–220. New York: Wiley.

Kothandapani, V. (1971). Validation of feeling, belief, and intention to act as three components of attitude and their contribution to prediction of contraceptive behavior. *Journal of Personality and Social Psychology*, **19**, 321–33.

Kuhl, J. (1985). Volitional aspect of achievement motivation and learned helplessness: Toward a comprehensive theory of action control. In B. A. Maher (Ed.), *Progress in experimental personality research*, Vol. 13, pp. 99–171. San Diego: Academic Press.

Lamb, C. W. and Stern, D. E., Jr (1978). An empirical validation of the randomized response technique. *Journal of Marketing Research*, **15**, 616–21.

LaPiere, R. T. (1934). Attitudes vs. actions. *Social Forces*, **13**, 230–7.

Lefcourt, H. M. (Ed.) (1981a). *Research with the locus of control construct. Vol. 1: Assessment methods*. San Diego: Academic Press.

Lefcourt, H. M. (1981b). Overview. In H. M. Lefcourt (Ed.), *Research with the locus of control construct. Vol. 1: Assessment methods*, pp. 1–11. San Diego: Academic Press.

Lefcourt, H. M. (1982). *Locus of control: Current trends in theory and research*, 2nd edition. Hillsdale, NJ: Lawrence Erlbaum Associates.

Lefcourt, H. M. (Ed.) (1983). *Research with the locus of control construct. Vol. 2: Developments and social problems*. San Diego: Academic Press.

Leon, G. R. and Roth, L. (1977). Obesity: Psychological causes, correlations, and speculations. *Psychological Bulletin*, **84**, 117–39.

Levenson, H. (1981). Differentiating among internality, powerful others, and chance. In H. M. Lefcourt (Ed.), *Research with the locus of control construct. Vol. 1: Assessment methods*, pp. 15–63. San Diego: Academic Press.

Likert, R. A. (1932). A technique for the measurement of attitudes. *Archives of Psychology*, **140**.

Liska, A. E. (1984). A critical examination of the causal structure of the Fishbein/Ajzen attitude–behavior model. *Social Psychology Quarterly*, **47**, 61–74.

Locke, E. A., Fredrick, E., Bobko, P. and Lee, C. (1984). Effect of self-efficacy, goals, and task strategies on task performance. *Journal of Applied Psychology*, **69**, 241–51.

Lord, C. G., Lepper, M. R. and Mackie, D. (1984). Attitude prototypes as determinants of attitude–behavior consistency. *Journal of Personality and Social Psychology*, **46**, 1254–66.

Lorr, M., O'Connor, J. P. and Seifert, R. F. (1977). A comparison of four personality inventories. *Journal of Personality Assessment*, **41**, 520–6.

Magnusson, D. (Ed.) (1981). *Toward a psychology of situations: An interactional perspective*. Hillsdale, NJ: Lawrence Erlbaum Associates.

Mann, R. D. (1959). A review of the relationships between personality and performance in small groups. *Psychological Bulletin*, **56**, 241–70.

Manstead, A. S. R., Proffitt, C. and Smart, J. L. (1983). Predicting and understanding mothers' infant-feeding intentions and behavior: Testing the theory of reasoned action. *Journal of Personality and Social Psychology*, **44**, 657–71.

McGowan, J. and Gormly, J. (1976). Validation of personality traits: A multicriteria approach. *Journal of Personality and Social Psychology*, **34**, 791–5.

McGuire, W. J. (1960a). Cognitive consistency and attitude change. *Journal of Abnormal and Social Psychology*, **60**, 345–53.

McGuire, W. J. (1960b). A syllogistic analysis of cognitive relationships. In C. I. Hovland and M. J. Rosenberg (Eds), *Attitude organization and change*, pp. 65–111. New Haven, CT: Yale University Press.

McGuire, W. J. (1969). The nature of attitudes and attitude change. In G. Lindzey and E. Aronson (Eds), *The handbook of social psychology*, 2nd edition, Vol. 3, pp. 136–314. Reading, MA: Addison-Wesley.

McGuire, W. J. (1985). Attitudes and attitude change. In G. Lindzey and E. Aronson (Eds), *Handbook of social psychology*, 3rd edition, Vol. 2, pp. 233–346. New York: Random House.

Merton, R. K. (1940). Fact and factitiousness in ethnic opinionnaires. *American Sociological Review*, **5**, 13–27.

Miller, G. A. (1956). The magical number seven plus or minus two: Some limits on our capacity for processing information. *Psychological Review*, **63**, 81–97.

Minard, R. D. (1952). Race relations in the Pocahontas coal field. *Journal of Social Issues*, **8**, 29–44.

Mischel, W. (1968). *Personality and assessment*. New York: Wiley.

Mischel, W. (1969). Continuity and change in personality. *American Psychologist*, **24**, 1012–28.

Mischel, W. (1983). Alternatives in the pursuit of the predictability and consistency of persons: Stable data that yield unstable interpretations. *Journal of Personality*, **51**, 578–604.

Mischel, W. (1984). Convergences and challenges in the search for consistency. *American Psychologist*, **39**, 351–64.

Mischel, W. and Peake, P. K. (1982a). Beyond *déjà vu* in the search for cross-situational consistency. *Psychological Review*, **89**, 730–55.

Mischel, W. and Peake, P. K. (1982b). In search of consistency: Measure for measure. In M. P. Zanna, E. T. Higgins and C. P. Herman (Eds), *Consistency in social behavior: The Ontario Symposium*, Vol. 2, pp. 187–207. Hillsdale, NJ: Lawrence Erlbaum Associates.

Monson, T. C., Hesley, J. W. and Chernick, L. (1982). Specifying when personality traits can and cannot predict behavior: An alternative to abandoning the attempt to predict single-act criteria. *Journal of Personality and Social Psychology*, **43**, 385–99.

Nisbett, R. E. (1977). Interaction versus main effects as goals of personality research. In D. Magnusson and N. S. Endler (Eds), *Personality at the crossroads: Current issues in interactional psychology*, pp. 235–41. New York: Wiley.

Nisbett, R. E. and Ross, L. (1980). *Human inference: Strategies and shortcomings of social judgment*. Englewood-Cliffs, NJ: Prentice-Hall.

Norman, R. (1975). Affective-cognitive consistency, attitudes, conformity, and behavior. *Journal of Personality and Social Psychology*, **32**, 83–91.

Norman, W. T. (1963). Toward an adequate taxonomy of personality attributes: Replicated factor structure in peer nomination personality ratings. *Journal of Abnormal and Social Psychology*, **66**, 574–83.

Olweus, D. (1979). Stability of aggressive reaction patterns in males: A review. *Psychological Bulletin*, **86**, 852–75.

Olweus, D. (1980). The consistency issue in personality psychology revisited – with special reference to aggression. *British Journal of Social and Clinical Psychology*, **19**, 377–90.

Osgood, C. E., Suci, G. J. and Tannenbaum, P. H. (1957). *The measurement of meaning*. Urbana, IL: University of Illinois Press.

Oskamp, S. (1977). *Attitudes and opinions*. Englewood-Cliffs, NJ: Prentice-Hall.

Ostrom, T. M. (1969). The relationship between the affective, behavioral, and cognitive components of attitude. *Journal of Experimental Social Psychology*, **5**, 12–30.

Parry, H. J. and Crossley, H. M. (1950). Validity of responses to survey questions. *Public Opinion Quarterly*, **14**, 61–80.

Peterson, D. R. (1968). *The clinical study of social behavior*. New York: Appleton-Century-Crofts.

Petty, R. E. and Cacioppo, J. T. (1981). *Attitudes and persuasion: Classic and contemporary approaches.* Dubuque, Iowa: Wm. C. Brown.

Petty, R. E. and Cacioppo, J. T. (1986). The Elaboration Likelihood Model of persuasion. In L. Berkowitz (Ed.), *Advances in experimental social psychology*, Vol. 19. San Diego: Academic Press.

Pomazal, R. J. and Jaccard, J. J. (1976). An informational approach to altruistic behavior. *Journal of Personality and Social Psychology*, 33, 317–26.

Pryor, J. B., Gibbons, F. X., Wicklund, R. A., Fazio, R. H. and Hood, R. (1977). Self-focused attention and self-report validity. *Journal of Personality*, 45, 514–27.

Raden, D. (1985). Strength-related attitude dimensions. *Social Psychology Quarterly*, 48, 312–30.

Regan, D. T. and Fazio, R. H. (1977). On the consistency between attitudes and behavior: Look to the method of attitude formation. *Journal of Experimental Social Psychology*, 13, 38–45.

Rosenberg, M. J. (1956). Cognitive structure and attitudinal affect. *Journal of Abnormal and Social Psychology*, 53, 367–72.

Rosenberg, M. J. (1960). An analysis of affective-cognitive consistency. In C. I. Hovland and M. J. Rosenberg (Eds), *Attitude organization and change*, pp. 15–64. New Haven: Yale University Press.

Rosenberg, M. J. (1965). Inconsistency arousal and reduction in attitude change. In I. D. Steiner and M. Fishbein (Eds), *Current studies in social psychology*, pp. 121–34. New York: Holt, Rinehart and Winston.

Rosenberg, M. J. (1968). Hedonism, inauthenticity, and other goals toward expansion of a consistency theory. In R. P. Abelson, E. Aronson, W. J. McGuire, T. M. Newcomb, M. J. Rosenberg and P. H. Tannenbaum (Eds). *Theories of cognitive consistency: A sourcebook*, pp. 73–111. Chicago: Rand McNally.

Rosenberg, M. J. and Hovland, C. I. (1960). Cognitive, affective, and behavioral components of attitudes. In C. I. Hovland and M. J. Rosenberg (Eds), *Attitude organization and change*, pp. 1–14. New Haven, CT: Yale University Press.

Roth, H. G. and Upmeyer, A. (1985). Matching attitudes towards cartoons across evaluative judgments and nonverbal evaluative behavior. *Psychological Research*, 47, 173–83.

Rotter, J. B. (1954). *Social learning and clinical psychology.* Englewood-Cliffs, NJ: Prentice-Hall.

Rotter, J. B. (1966). Generalized expectancies for internal versus external control of reinforcement. *Psychological Monographs*, 80, 1 (Whole No. 609).

Rundquist, E. A. and Sletto, R. F. (1936). *Personality in the depression.* Minneapolis: University of Minnesota Press.

Rushton, J. P., Brainerd, C. J. and Pressley, M. (1983). Behavioral development and construct validity: The principle of aggregation. *Psychological Bulletin*, **94**, 18–38.

Sample, J. and Warland, R. (1973). Attitude and prediction of behavior. *Social Forces*, **51**, 292–303.

Sanger, S. P. and Alker, H. A. (1972). Dimensions of internal–external locus of control and the women's liberation movement. *Journal of Social Issues*, **28**, 115–29.

Sarver, V. T., Jr (1983). Ajzen and Fishbein's "theory of reasoned action": A critical assessment. *Journal for the Theory of Social Behavior*, **13**, 155–63.

Scheier, M. F., Buss, A. H. and Buss, D. M. (1978). Self-consciousness, self-report of aggressiveness, and aggression. *Journal of Research in Personality*, **12**, 133–40.

Schifter, D. B. and Ajzen, I. (1985). Intention, perceived control, and weight loss: An application of the theory of planned behavior. *Journal of Personality and Social Psychology*, **49**, 843–51.

Schlegel, R. P. (1975). Multidimensional measurement of attitude towards smoking marijuana. *Canadian Journal of Behavioral Science*, **7**, 387–96.

Schlegel, R. P. and DiTecco, D. (1982). Attitudinal structures and the attitude–behavior relation. In M. P. Zanna, E. T. Higgins and C. P. Herman (Eds), *Consistency in social behavior: The Ontario Symposium*, Vol. 2, pp. 17–49. Hillsdale, NJ: Lawrence Erlbaum Associates.

Schuman, H. and Johnson, M. P. (1976). Attitudes and behavior. *Annual Review of Sociology*, **2**, 161–207.

Schwartz, S. H. (1977). Normative influences on altruism. In L. Berkowitz (Ed.), *Advances in experimental social psychology*, Vol. 10, pp. 221–79. San Diego: Academic Press.

Sejwacz, D., Ajzen, I. and Fishbein, M. (1980). Predicting and understanding weight loss: Intentions, behaviors, and outcomes. In I. Ajzen and M. Fishbein (Eds), *Understanding attitudes and predicting social behavior*, pp. 101–12. Englewood-Cliffs, NJ: Prentice-Hall.

Sherif, M. and Hovland, C. I. (1961). *Social judgment: Assimilation and contrast effects in communication and attitude change*. New Haven, CT: Yale University Press.

Sherman, S. J. and Fazio, R. H. (1983). Parallels between attitudes and traits as predictors of behavior. *Journal of Personality*, **51**, 308–45.

Shweder, R. A. (1975). How relevant is an individual difference theory of personality? *Journal of Personality*, **43**, 455–85.

Sivacek, J. and Crano, W. D. (1982). Vested interest as a moderator of attitude–behavior consistency. *Journal of Personality and Social Psychology*, **43**, 210–21.

Sjöberg, L. (1982). Attitude–behavior correlation, social desirability and perceived diagnostic value. *British Journal of Social Psychology*, **21**, 283–92.

Small, S. A., Zeldin, R. S. and Savin-Williams, R. C. (1983). In search of personality traits: A multimethod analysis of naturally occurring prosocial and dominance behavior. *Journal of Personality*, **51**, 1–16.

Smetana, J. G. and Adler, N. E. (1980). Fishbein's value x expectancy model: An examination of some assumptions. *Personality and Social Psychology Bulletin*, **6**, 89–96.

Smith, M. B. (1947). The personal setting of public opinions: A study of attitudes toward Russia. *Public Opinion Quarterly*, **11**, 507–23.

Snyder, M. (1974). The self-monitoring of expressive behavior. *Journal of Personality and Social Psychology*, **30**, 526–37.

Snyder, M. (1979). Self-monitoring processes. In L. Berkowitz (Ed.), *Advances in experimental social psychology*, Vol. 12, pp. 85–128. San Diego: Academic Press.

Snyder, M. (1982). When believing means doing: Creating links between attitudes and behavior. In M. P. Zanna, E. T. Higgins and C. P. Herman (Eds), *Consistency in social behavior: The Ontario symposium*, Vol. 2, pp. 105–30. Hillsdale, NJ: Lawrence Erlbaum Associates.

Snyder, M. and Kendzierski, D. (1982). Acting on one's attitudes: Procedures for linking attitude and behavior. *Journal of Experimental Social Psychology*, **18**, 165–83.

Snyder, M. and Swann, W. B., Jr (1976). When actions reflect attitudes: The politics of impression management. *Journal of Personality and Social Psychology*, **34**, 1034–42.

Songer-Nocks, E. (1976a). Situational factors affecting the weighting of predictor components in the Fishbein model. *Journal of Experimental Social Psychology*, **12**, 56–69.

Songer-Nocks, E. (1976b). Reply to Fishbein and Ajzen. *Journal of Experimental Social Psychology*, **12**, 585–90.

Sroufe, L. A. (1979). The coherence of individual development: Early care, attachment, and subsequent developmental issues. *American Psychologist*, **34**, 834–41.

Sroufe, L. A. and Waters, E. (1977). Attachment as an organizational construct. *Child Development*, **48**, 1184–99.

Staub, E. (1974). Helping a distressed person: Social, personality, and stimulus determinants. In L. Berkowitz (Ed.), *Advances in experimental social psychology*, Vol. 10, pp. 293–341. San Diego: Academic Press.

Tedeschi, J. T., Schlenker, B. R. and Bonoma, T. V. (1971). Cognitive dissonance: Private ratiocination or public spectacle. *American Psychologist*, **26**, 685–95.

Tellegen, A., Kamp, J. and Watson, D. (1982). Recognizing individual differences in predictive structure. *Psychological Review*, **89**, 95–105.

Thurstone, L. L. (1931). The measurement of attitudes. *Journal of Abnormal and Social Psychology*, **26**, 249–69.

Thurstone, L. L. and Chave, E. J. (1929). *The measurement of attitude.* Chicago: University of Chicago Press.

Tittle, C. R. and Hill, R. J. (1967). Attitude measurement and prediction of behavior: An evaluation of conditions and measurement techniques. *Sociometry*, 30, 199–213.

Triandis, H. C. (1977). *Interpersonal behavior.* Monterey, CA: Brooks/ Cole.

Underwood, B. and Moore, B. S. (1981). Sources of behavioral consistency. *Journal of Personality and Social Psychology*, 40, 780–5.

Upmeyer, A. (1981). Perceptual and judgmental processes in social contexts. In L. Berkowitz (Ed.), *Advances in experimental social psychology*, Vol. 14, pp. 257–308. San Diego: Academic Press.

Veevers, J. E. (1971). Drinking attitudes and drinking behavior: An exploratory study. *Journal of Social Psychology*, 85, 103–9.

Vernon, P. E. (1964). *Personality assessment: A critical survey.* New York: Wiley.

Vinokur, A. and Caplan, R. D. (1987). Attitudes and social support: Determinants of job-seeking behavior and well-being among the unemployed. *Journal of Applied Social Psychology*, 18, 1007–24.

Vinokur, A., Caplan, R. D., and Williams, C. C. (1987). Effects of recent and past stress on mental health: Coping with unemployment among Vietnam veterans and nonveterans. *Journal of Applied Social Psychology*, 17, 710–30.

Vinokur-Kaplan, D. (1978). To have – or not to have – another child: Family planning attitudes, intentions, and behavior. *Journal of Applied Social Psychology*, 8, 29–46.

Wallston, B. S., Wallston, K. A., Kaplan, G. D. and Maides, S. A. (1976). Development and validation of the health locus of control (HLC) scale. *Journal of Consulting and Clinical Psychology*, 44, 580–5.

Wallston, K. A. and Wallston, B. S. (1981). Health locus of control scales. In H. M. Lefcourt (Ed.), *Research with the locus of control construct. Vol. 1: Assessment methods*, pp. 189–243. San Diego: Academic Press.

Wallston, K. A., Wallston, B. S., and DeVellis, R. (1978). Development of the multidimensional health locus of control (MHLC) scales. *Health Education Monographs*, 6, 161–70.

Warehime, R. G. (1972). Generalized expectancy for locus of control and academic performance. *Psychological Reports*, 30, 314.

Warland, R. H. and Sample, J. (1973). Response certainty as a moderator variable in attitude measurement. *Rural Sociology*, 38, 174–86.

Warner, L. G. and DeFleur, M. L. (1969). Attitude as an interactional concept: Social constraint and social distance as intervening variables between attitudes and action. *American Sociological Review*, 34, 153–69.

Warner, S. L. (1965). Randomized response: A survey technique for eliminating evasive answer bias. *Journal of the American Statistical Association*, 60, 63–9.

Waters, E. (1978). The reliability and stability of individual differences in infant–mother attachment. *Child Development*, 49, 483–94.

Weigel, R. H. and Newman, L. S. (1976). Increasing attitude–behavior correspondence by broadening the scope of the behavioral measure. *Journal of Personality and Social Psychology*, 33, 793–802.

Weigel, R. H., Vernon, D. T. A. and Tognacci, L. N. (1974). The specificity of the attitude as a determinant of attitude–behavior congruence. *Journal of Personality and Social Psychology*, 30, 724–8.

Werner, P. D. (1978). Personality and attitude–activism correspondence. *Journal of Personality and Social Psychology*, 36, 1375–90.

Wicker, A. W. (1969). Attitudes versus actions: The relationship of verbal and overt behavioral responses to attitude objects. *Journal of Social Issues*, 25, 41–78.

Wicklund, R. A. (1975). Objective self awareness. In L. Berkowitz (Ed.), *Advances in experimental social psychology*, vol. 8, pp. 233–75. San Diego: Academic Press.

Widaman, K. F. (1985). Hierarchically nested covariance structure models for multitrait–multimethod data. *Applied Psychological Measurement*, 9, 1–26.

Wiggins, J. S. (1973). *Personality and prediction: Principles of personality assessment*. Reading, MA: Addison-Wesley.

Wilson, T. D. and Dunn, D. S. (1986). Effects of introspection on attitude–behavior consistency. Analyzing reasons versus focusing on feelings. *Journal of Experimental Social Psychology*, 22, 249–63.

Wilson, T. D., Dunn, D. S., Bybee, J. A., Hyman, D. B. and Rotondo, J. A. (1984). Effects of analyzing reasons on attitude–behavior consistency. *Journal of Personality and Social Psychology*, 47, 5–16.

Wright, J. C. (1983). *The structure and perception of behavioral consistency*. Unpublished doctoral dissertation. Stanford University.

Zajonc, R. B. (1968). Cognitive theories in social psychology. In G. Lindzey and E. Aronson (Eds), *The handbook of social psychology*, 2nd edition, Vol. 1, pp. 320–411. Reading, MA: Addison-Wesley.

Zanna, M. P., Olson, J. M., and Fazio, R. H. (1980). Attitude–behavior consistency: An individual difference perspective. *Journal of Personality and Social Psychology*, 38, 432–40.

Zedeck, S. (1971). Problems with the use of "moderator" variables. *Psychological Bulletin*, 76, 295–310.

Zuckerman, M. and Reis, H. T. (1978). Comparison of three models for predicting altruistic behavior. *Journal of Personality and Social Psychology*, 36, 498–510.

# AUTHOR INDEX

# SUBJECT INDEX

Personality Research Form, 52
personality scales, 17
personality traits
  definition of, 2, 7
  dimensions, 19–20
  and driving, 40
  explanatory value of, 109–110
  and leadership, 40
  as moderating variables, 67–71
  and specific actions, 39–41,
    92–3, 98–107
  types of, 30
  and weight loss, 40–1
  see also specific traits
persuasion, 26
physical activity, 56–7
physiological reactions see
  measurement
political attitudes, 1, 31, 68
political involvement, 104
prediction see behavior
predictive validity, 37–41
  for behavioral aggregates, 54–7
prior behavior see past behavior
prisoner's dilemma game, 108
privacy, 81, 83
pro-social behavior, 53
psychological research, attitudes
  toward, 69, 72, 76, 78
punctuality, 36, 51
punishment, attitude toward, 82,
  87

racial attitudes, 39, 81
referents, 121, 125
reflection about attitudes, 73–4
relevance of behavior, 84–5
reliability (of measurement), 10, 12,
  36, 57–8
religiosity, 1, 14, 18, 37–8, 52, 54,
  84, 86, 120
representativeness (of
  measurement), 18, 85
resistance to temptation, 36
responses
  nonverbal, 1–2, 4–7, 21, 23, 38,
    53, 56, 149
  overt, 2–3, 27, 146–7

verbal, 2–3, 4–7, 21, 23, 38,
    149
response tendencies, 23, 46, 47–8,
  50, 54, 63, 95, 98, 147
  temporal stability of, 99–101
Rorschach method, 4

salience see attitude, salience of;
  beliefs, salience of
self-awareness, 82, 87–8
self-consciousness, 15, 85
  as a moderating variable, 69–70
self-efficacy expectations, 105–6;
  see also perceived behavioral
  control
self-monitoring tendency, 67–9,
  86–7
self-reports of behavior, 3, 8, 23,
  52, 56, 70, 147
  and actual behavior, 102–3
semantic differential, 10–11, 21,
  52, 72
single-act index, 47, 48–9, 58,
  94
situational constraints, 81–2
situational factors
  effects on behavior, 35
  as moderating variables, 80–3
skill, and volitional control, 128–9
smoking, attitude toward, 1, 68
snakes, attitude toward, 22, 31,
  56
sociability, 1, 3–4, 20, 23, 70, 82,
  94–5; see also introversion-
  extraversion
social desirability, 102, 149
Socratic effect, 31
Spearman–Brown prophesy
  formula, 12, 47
stability of behavior, 50–1, 53,
  148; see also response
  tendencies; temporal stability
stereotypes, 97–8
subjective norm, 117–18
submissiveness see dominance
syllogisms, 31

target element, 94–5, 96–8